The Elevated Leader

ENDORSEMENTS

"In our rapidly evolving world, elevated leadership service is needed more than ever to create working together environments with all the stakeholders to create value for all and the greater good. Ryan presents a very compelling vision, strategy, and plan to take our leadership to the next level of performance and service."

Alan Mulally

Former CEO of Boeing Commercial Airplanes
and the Ford Motor Company

"I often get asked how one can strengthen their "positivity muscles." This book presents cutting-edge ideas from psychology and neuroscience to teach you how to do just that. It's a must read if you want to learn how to lift yourself up so you can lift others up!"

Jon Gordon

13x best-selling author of *The Energy Bus* and
Power of Positive Leadership

"Becoming our better future self requires upgrading our internal operating system, and this book clearly and powerfully explains how you can do that."

Dr. Benjamin Hardy

Author of *Be Your Future Self Now*

THE ELEVATED LEADER

LEVEL UP YOUR LEADERSHIP THROUGH
VERTICAL DEVELOPMENT

RYAN GOTTFREDSON

NEW YORK

LONDON • NASHVILLE • MELBOURNE • VANCOUVER

THE ELEVATED LEADER

Level Up Your Leadership Through Vertical Development

Published in New York, New York, by Morgan James Publishing. Morgan James is a trademark of Morgan James, LLC. www.MorganJamesPublishing.com

Proudly distributed by Ingram Publisher Services.

A **FREE** ebook edition is available for you or a friend with the purchase of this print book.

CLEARLY SIGN YOUR NAME ABOVE

Instructions to claim your free ebook edition:
1. Visit MorganJamesBOGO.com
2. Sign your name CLEARLY in the space above
3. Complete the form and submit a photo of this entire page
4. You or your friend can download the ebook to your preferred device

ISBN 9781631958915 paperback
ISBN 9781631958922 ebook
Library of Congress Control Number: 2022931987

Cover Design by:
Rupert Reyneke
www.redstonestudio.com

Interior Design by:
Chris Treccani
www.3dogcreative.net

Morgan James is a proud partner of Habitat for Humanity Peninsula and Greater Williamsburg. Partners in building since 2006.

Get involved today! Visit MorganJamesPublishing.com/giving-back

TABLE OF CONTENTS

FREE DIGITAL VERTICAL DEVELOPMENT COACH

I am beyond excited to partner with Qstream, a training and development software company, to provide you with the Digital Vertical Development Coach, a free tool that goes along with this book.

How many times have you attended a training or read a book and almost immediately forgot everything you just learned? Qstream specializes in providing microlearning and knowledge reinforcement tools to help you deepen your personal development and retain information.

The Digital Vertical Development Coach was designed to help you in these ways:

1. Facilitate your vertical development
2. Master and retain the material covered in this book
3. Deepen your self-awareness, including understanding how you think and learn
4. Help you to be more intentional about your leadership

After you enroll in the Digital Vertical Development Coach, you will receive regular emails (about three days a week) inviting you to engage in three short questions or exercises. These are designed to take approximately ten minutes.

There are thirty such questions/exercises. When you complete one correctly, that question or exercise will pop up again approximately four weeks later. When you complete a question/exercise incorrectly, it will pop up again approximately two weeks later. Once you get it right twice in a row, that question/exercise is considered mastered, and it will become inactive.

These exercises serve as short interventions that, when repeated over time, will produce the benefits listed above. The approach is aligned with the latest neuroscientific research that suggests upgrading the wiring in your mind requires small, repeated interventions.

Generally, Qstream charges organizations or individuals for enrollment in their microlearning tools, but for this book, they have graciously allowed me to offer it to you for free.

I believe if you use this tool, you will sense the power of Qstream and see how their approach will not only benefit your personal growth and development, but how your organization could use Qstream to support any training and development initiative.

To download the tool, go to www.qstream.com/TheElevatedLeader, or use the following QR code:

WHY THIS BOOK IS NEEDED NOW MORE THAN EVER

Do you want to learn how to better elevate other leaders, your team, or yourself so they and you have a higher-level impact? If so, you are in the right place.

On at least one level, you can probably resonate with Michael, one of my clients. Michael is the head of talent and development for a large multinational organization. He is a dynamic and purpose-fueled person and leader.

If you were to question Michael about his purpose, he would give you a clear answer. In fact, he would tell you that he has *three* purposes.

His first purpose is to elevate the leaders within his organization. This is a priority for him because Michael recognizes that his organization's leaders are facing increasing change, pressure, uncertainty, and complexity, and if he can help those leaders enhance their capacity to navigate these circumstances, the organization will be able to navigate into the future with greater effectiveness and agility. As such, Michael is on a mission to raise the entire organization by elevating its leaders.

His second purpose is to elevate his team of eight direct reports. One of his biggest desires is to help his employees reach their potential. Thus, it is a priority for him to invest in their development. Michael sees two benefits to elevating his team, believing first that an elevated team communicates more effectively, makes better decisions, and does better and more sophisticated work. He also believes the more elevated his team members are, the more he can trust them. When this trust is there, the work goes more smoothly. He does not have to micromanage, which allows him to focus more on big-picture, important tasks and less on smaller-picture, urgent tasks. By elevating his team, not only will they perform at a higher level, but it will allow Michael to spend more of his time and resources on personally making a bigger and deeper contribution to his organization.

His third purpose is to elevate himself. Michael wants to be the best leader he can be. He knows that if he wants to elevate his organization and his team, he must first elevate himself. The more elevated he is, the more he will be the positive, uplifting influence he desires to be.

Michael also recognizes that the benefits of elevating himself extend beyond his work life. He knows the more elevated he is, the greater his influence could be across *all* areas of his life, including with his family. Michael is on a mission to be the best person he can be and make the most out of the journey of life.

Are you like Michael? Do you have a strong desire to elevate other leaders, your team, or yourself? If so, I commend you. But I am also aware that you may have encountered some frustrations, just as Michael has.

While Michael has clear desires around elevating his organization, his team, and himself, he has found making this happen is easier said than done.

THE PROBLEMS

There are some limitations in the leadership development space that prevent us from being successful at elevating our leaders, our teams, or ourselves. Until we acknowledge and address those, we'll find ourselves on the hamster wheel of development, where we feel like we are working hard to create change and improvement, but we are only seeing small, incremental improvements instead of the transformational change that we desire.

Some of these limitations are problems that we already recognize and acknowledge. We can refer to these as "known, spoken problems." Other limitations are problems that we recognize but are hesitant to acknowledge. We can refer to these as "known, unspoken problems." Finally, there are limitations that most leaders do not recognize and they are, therefore, rarely talked about. We can refer to these as "unknown, unspoken problems."

Let me highlight some of these problems in the leadership development space, for once we recognize them, we can do something about them.

Known, Spoken Problems

In *Mastering Leadership*, authors Robert J. Anderson and William A. Adams state, "The development of leadership effectiveness must, at a minimum, keep pace with the rate of change and the rate of escalating complexity."

Unfortunately, the development of leadership effectiveness is not keeping pace with the rate of change and escalating complexity. And therein lies a massive problem.

Organizations are facing market conditions that include increasing competition, shortening product life cycles, and rapidly changing customer interests and needs. And these conditions seem to only be intensifying.

What this means for us as leaders is that—ready or not—we have to navigate change, pressure, uncertainty, and complexity that is often more than what we are cognitively and emotionally prepared to handle. As a result, we are running at a leadership deficit, and that deficit is growing.

Just how problematic this is will become more apparent as we jump into the known, unspoken problems.

Known, Unspoken Problems

There are two primary known, unspoken problems with leadership development: most leaders are not very effective, and leadership development is largely broken. These are two sides of the same coin.

Unfortunately, research on leadership effectiveness does not paint a pretty picture. Consider the following:

1. Development Dimensions International reported that 60 percent of employees acknowledge their boss damages their self-esteem.
2. Positive change consultant Michelle McQuaid, PhD, found that 65 percent of employees said that having a better boss would make them happier than getting a pay raise.
3. Gallup found that in the United States, a meager 36 percent of employees were found to be engaged in their work, and managers account for 70 percent of the variance in employee engagement.
4. Gallup also reported that when it comes to performance reviews, a meager 14 percent of employees strongly agree the reviews they received inspired them to improve, just 20 percent of employees strongly agree their performance was managed in a way that motivated them to do outstanding work, and only 26 percent of employees strongly agreed their manager continually helped them clarify priorities.

Hogan, a leadership assessment organization, reported that 75 percent of employees say their immediate supervisor is the most stressful part of their job.

These statistics point to a harsh reality: Most leaders do not seem to be doing a great job.

To add fuel to the fire, it does not seem that typical leadership development efforts are helping leaders develop and become more effective. TrainingIndustry.com estimated that organizations worldwide spend $366 billion a year on leadership development. Despite such a huge investment, the BrandonHall Group found that 75 percent of organizations rated their leadership development programs as not very effective, and 71 percent of organizations did not feel their leaders were able to lead their organization into the future.

These findings are all based on data from 2015. Given the rise in uncertainty and complexity associated with the COVID-19 pandemic, I believe these statistics would be even worse today.

Clearly, it appears that organizations are not getting a very good return on their investment in leadership development.

The message seems clear to me: Leaders are not as effective as we would like them to be, and leadership development, as it now stands, neither elevates nor transforms the effectiveness of leaders.

This is not due to a lack of effort. Leaders seem to be trying their best. Plus, most leadership development programs are well-intended and well thought out.

So, what are we doing wrong?

This is where an unknown, unspoken problem comes into play.

The Unknown, Unspoken Problem

There is an unknown, unspoken problem hiding in plain sight. Few recognize it and fully appreciate its implications.

The focus of this book is on uncovering and solving this problem in leadership development. I will identify the problem and solution at a high level now, and then we will dive into these in great depth throughout the book.

To understand the unknown, unspoken problem and its solution, we need to recognize that there are two forms of leadership development: horizontal development and vertical development.

The unknown, unspoken problem is that over the last seventy years of leadership development, when leadership developers and researchers have talked or written about development, they have primarily been referring to *horizontal* development.

Horizontal development focuses on improving a leader's knowledge, skills, and abilities. It is a valuable form of development because it allows leaders to do more than what they were able to do previously. It broadens their functionality. For example, if a student were to take an accounting course, that student is expected to gain knowledge and skills so that once they have completed the course, they are able to succeed at accounting jobs. In taking the course, the student has broadened their functionality.

This would be similar to downloading an app onto an iPad or smartphone. The new app allows the device to do more than what it could do previously. Using the example above, an accounting course is the app that is being downloaded onto the student.

When it comes to the horizontal development of leaders, commonly provided apps come in the form of leadership styles, delivering feedback, conflict resolution, dealing with change, and leading innovation. The list goes on. Generally, all of these efforts focus on improving our knowledge, skills, and abilities.

While such horizontal development efforts can be helpful, they have a severe limitation.

In the case of an iPad, while a new app may broaden its functionality, it neither improves the device's effectiveness nor its efficiency. Adding an app does not allow the device to take on more complex or sophisticated tasks. In fact, the addition of a new app may cause the iPad to slow down.

The same is true of the college student taking an accounting course. Just because they gain knowledge and skills about accounting does not mean they are any more capable of navigating the stress, pressure, uncertainty, and complexity of life in general.

Whether we want an iPad or a person to improve in how they operate as a whole, they need a different form of development. They need vertical development.

Vertical development is not about helping a leader *do more*; it is about helping the leader *be better*. It is not focused on simply downloading new knowledge, skills, or abilities onto a person; it is about upgrading their internal operating system, such that they operate and navigate life at a higher level.

The technical definition of **vertical development is elevating a leader's ability to make meaning of their world in more cognitively and emotionally sophisticated ways.**

Everyone has an internal operating system. Our internal operating systems dictate how we see and make meaning of our world.

In fact, it is theoretically possible to line people up in order of how cognitively and emotionally sophisticated their internal operating system is. People at the low end of the line might make meaning of constructive criticism as an attack and are prone to get defensive. They may also make meaning of vulnerability as a sign of weakness. People at the high end of the line, though, make meaning of these things in more cognitively and emotionally sophisticated ways. Specifically, they are more likely to make meaning of constructive criticism as an opportunity to learn and grow and vulnerability as a signal of strength.

The people with more elevated internal operating systems, those who make meaning of their world in more cognitively and emotionally sophisticated ways, function at a higher level, and they have a greater capacity to navigate change, pressure, uncertainty, and complexity.

Thus, vertical development is all about shifting someone's place along this theoretical line. This type of development focuses on upgrading a leader's internal operating system so they are programmed to see and make meaning of their world in more cognitively and emotionally sophisticated ways. In doing so, they navigate life and lead at a higher, more effective level.

* * *

The vast majority of leadership development—upwards of 95 percent of all such efforts—primarily focuses on horizontal development. Offering these leaders apps in the form of knowledge, skills, and abilities is only incrementally helpful.

xviii | THE ELEVATED LEADER

This focus on horizontal development and the lack of vertical development is what has led to the known spoken and known unspoken problems of leadership.

Not only is horizontal development incapable of helping leaders develop at a pace that matches or exceeds the rising complexity in their world, but it has also led to subpar leadership effectiveness. And it has led to ineffective leadership development efforts.

If we want to change this somber reality, if we want to elevate ourselves and the leaders we work with, we need vertical development.

The focus of this book is entirely on helping you understand what vertical development is, why vertical development is essential, and how you can develop vertically.

Not only will you see that vertical development is the answer to our biggest leadership problems; you will be empowered to unlock the power of vertical development to elevate leaders, your team, and yourself.

WHY RYAN?

With any non-fiction book, you should be asking yourself, "Why should I lend an ear to this author? Why should I trust them?"

While I am not the only person teaching and speaking on this topic, my approach to vertical development is different from that of others I have studied.

My experience is a unique blend of an academic and applied approach to leadership development. I am an associate professor of leadership at California State University, Fullerton, where I am a part of the second-largest business school in the United States. As a professor, I have researched leadership for over ten years, and to date, I have published over twenty peer-reviewed articles across some of the top academic journals in management.

I am also a leadership consultant. I started consulting at Gallup, a preeminent management consulting company, during a self-chosen one-year leave of absence from Cal State Fullerton. Upon returning to the university, I started a consulting company focused on helping organizations develop their leaders and employees through a focus on mindsets. This opened the door for me to work with top leaders at organizations all over the world, including CVS Health, Deutsche Telekom, Mondelez, Ford, Circle K, Cook Medical, and dozens of others spanning nearly all industries.

As a researcher and consultant, I am concerned about providing organizations and leaders with research-backed information, but I also know that I need to do so in a way that is both powerful and approachable. I believe this book blends research and practice in a manner that is approachable, powerful, and engaging.

I also bring three unique perspectives to the topic of vertical development that I believe are unparalleled.

First, to understand my unique perspective toward vertical development, it is helpful to know a little bit about the history of vertical development. The term *vertical development* is relatively new, but the concepts behind it have been studied for over fifty years under the domains of developmental psychology, humanistic psychology, adult development, and psychological maturity.

Over the last fifty years, researchers and thought leaders have developed a variety of vertical development frameworks and hierarchies that identify different levels or stages of vertical development. Some of the primary researchers and thought leaders in the space of vertical development include Abraham Maslow, Robert Kegan, Jane Loevinger, Lawrence Kohlberg, Terri O'Fallon, Suzanne Cook-Greuter, William Torbert, Antionette Braks, and Nick Petrie.

As I studied each of the frameworks developed by these thought leaders, three things became apparent. First, each of them brought unique insights to the concept of vertical development. Second, their frameworks identify a different number of hierarchical levels. The fewest levels I have seen is three, and the most I have seen is twelve. Third, despite there being different frameworks with differing numbers of levels, all agree that there are three base levels.

How I differ from the other researchers and thought leaders in this space is I am not beholden to any thought leader or any single one of their frameworks. What I have done with this book is to take the best ideas from each of the thought leaders and their frameworks and present the three levels of vertical development that all experts seem to agree upon. I believe that by taking this broad approach to vertical development, I have compiled the most comprehensive view on the topic.

A second unique perspective that I bring to the field of vertical development is that I am a mindset expert. In my *Wall Street Journal* and *USA Today* best-selling book, *Success Mindsets*, I introduced the most comprehensive and research-backed mindset framework ever compiled. This is significant because when we recognize that vertical development is all about how cognitively and emotionally sophisticated we see the world and make meaning of it, it is easy to see that vertical development foundationally involves a focus on mindsets. Despite this fact, I have not come across a vertical development expert that focuses on mindsets with the depth and precision that I do.

This brings us to the third unique perspective I bring to the vertical development space: neuroscience. To understand exactly what mindsets are and the role they play in our lives, I have had to become an expert on the neuroscience behind mindsets. This has led to some important discoveries.

First, I found that neuroscience identifies mindsets as the most foundational aspect for why we do what we do. Next, I discovered how our mindsets are developed and how they change at a neurological level. This discovery led me to develop an expertise on trauma and the role it has on our brains, neurological systems, mindsets, and, as a result, our vertical development.

Because I cover the comprehensive breadth of vertical development thought and include the depth of mindsets and neuroscience, I believe this is the most comprehensive book on vertical development written to date. The benefit of this is that I believe it has great potential to empower you to elevate who you are as a leader as well as elevate those you lead and work with.

HOW TO USE THIS BOOK

In the first half of the book, we will cover what vertical development is, expand on why vertical development is so important, and identify and describe the three mind levels. By reading this section, you should be able to get a clear sense of your current vertical altitude and identify a higher vertical altitude you can elevate into, which sets the stage for the second half of the book.

The second half of the book focuses on how we develop vertically. It provides clear practical guidance on how you can rewire your internal operating system and heal your mind, and how you can help others do the same.

To help you get the most out of this book and accelerate your own vertical development, there are some tools and resources that I am making available to you.

Personal Assessments

At two points in the book, I will invite you to take two different personal assessments. The first is a vertical development assessment designed to help you identify your current vertical altitude. The second is a mindset assessment designed to help you identify the quality of your mindsets across four sets of mindsets. Together, these assessments will help you deepen your self-awareness and identify opportunities and areas for vertical development. These come free to you. As you read through the book, you will be directed on when and where you can complete these assessments.

Digital Vertical Development Coach

In partnership with Qstream, a cutting-edge microlearning and knowledge retention solution, we are providing you with free access to a groundbreaking personal development and learning retention tool that has never been provided with a book before. We call this tool a Digital

Vertical Development Coach. There are two primary benefits to using the Digital Vertical Development Coach.

First, it will help you retain the content this book covers. Research has found that within four weeks of reading a book, the average person tends to forget more than 80 percent of what they had read. However, Qstream did research in partnership with Harvard and found that by engaging with Qstream's unique neuroscience-based methodology and using the Digital Vertical Development Coach, you can exponentially increase your retention of the content covered in this book. In fact, their research found users to recall 170 percent more than traditional learning.

Second, it will help you develop vertically. As you go through this book, you will see that to develop vertically, you must rewire your mind. The Digital Vertical Development Coach is the perfect tool to help you do this.

As you will read, vertical development occurs when we improve our mindsets and make meaning of our world in more cognitively and emotionally sophisticated ways. Our mindsets, at a neurological level, are neural connections. And neural connections are a lot like muscles: The more you exercise them, the stronger they become. Thus, to develop vertically, we effectively need to hit the gym for our mind. The Digital Vertical Development Coach is that gym.

Specifically, the Digital Vertical Development Coach provides you with regular workouts specifically geared to strengthen the positive mindset neural connections identified and promoted in this book.

If you choose to use this tool, you will be invited to engage in vertical development exercises three times a week. These exercises will come to you either by email or app, and they will include questions, videos, and short journaling activities.

You will be sent three exercises at a time, three days a week. These will take approximately ten to fifteen minutes to complete.

Every time you successfully complete one exercise, that exercise will pop up again about four weeks later. You will be required to successfully complete an exercise *twice* for it to be retired. If you do not successfully complete an exercise, that exercise will pop up again two weeks later. Depending on your mastery level, completing all thirty exercises will take about two months.

Digital Vertical Development Coach users have reported increased self-awareness and meta-cognition as well as greater intentionality about their mindsets and their life, leadership, and influence. One user of the Digital Vertical Development Coach wrote me recently, saying,

I decided to leave my ego behind on this one . . . [and] buy the Digital Vertical Development Coach. It was one of the best decisions I made this year. The content is rich and the methodology to repeat questions and so on seems to work well. I feel I am progressing . . . My behavior is changing . . . [and] I am feeling more relaxed with the idea of being wrong and being more open to seek feedback and do not get stuck with my own ideas. I am reaching out to people with humility. [I am] becoming conscious that I have a lot to learn and that there is a long and promising way ahead for me to improve my mindset [so I can] reach better outcomes in my personal and professional life.

To download your free copy of the Digital Vertical Development Coach, go to www.Qstream.com/TheElevatedLeader.

Are you ready to begin your vertical development journey? Let's do this.

PART ONE

Vertical Development and
the Three Mind Levels

CHAPTER ONE

THE KEY TO UNLOCKING TRUE LEADERSHIP TRANSFORMATION

Vertical Development Law #1
Leaders make meaning of their world at different levels of cognitive and emotional sophistication.

We need elevated leaders now more than ever before. The state of leadership is in a precarious situation, and organizations are increasingly finding themselves running on a leadership deficit.

In 2020, we were already recognizing that leaders were facing escalating change, pressure, uncertainty, and complexity. Then the COVID-19 pandemic hit, and these factors skyrocketed. As the COVID-19 pandemic wanes, organizations are taking stock of the situation, and they are finding the change, pressure, uncertainty, and complexity their leaders are facing exceeds their leaders' current capacities to effectively navigate these tumultuous conditions. Hence, the leadership deficit.

The deficiencies associated with organizational leadership were confirmed well before the COVID-19 pandemic. In 2015, the BrandonHall Group found that **71 percent of organizations do not feel their leaders can lead their organization into the future, and 75 percent of organi-**

zations rate their leadership development programs as not being very effective. I would imagine these percentages are even higher today.

As a leadership development professional, what has been shocking to me is that while organizational leaders certainly *feel* this deficit, they rarely recognize what the problem is, how big of an issue it is, and what to do about it.

Let me give you an example. I received a phone call from a university president asking me to do a workshop with her leadership team. She described a laundry list of problems in her organization, including a decrease in enrollment, the threat of a teacher strike, and her leadership team being burned out from all of the changes they have had to navigate over the last several years.

When I asked her how she thought I could best help her, she suggested that her leaders needed "an inspirational pick-me-up," a pep talk. While I could easily offer that, I told her that doing so would be like offering a Band-Aid for a gaping wound, And I would prefer to help her address the wound. She disagreed with my evaluation, arguing that there was no wound; her staff was simply fatigued.

What she could not see nor *wanted* to see was that their tumultuous situation exceeded their level of development. A pep talk might make them feel better for a moment, but it would not improve their capacity to navigate their challenging environment. It would neither elevate their leadership capacity, nor would it do anything to increase enrollment, prevent a strike, or address staff burnout.

That university is no outlier. I have found this dynamic playing out in many, if not most, of the organizations I work with. Leaders are telling me they are tired of dealing with constant change. While not fully realizing it, what they are essentially saying is that the demands associated with their responsibilities as a leader are heavier than what they can currently carry.

Perhaps you can relate. If you were to rate your current state as a leader on a scale from suffering to struggling to surviving to thriving, where would you place yourself? And where would you rate the leaders around you?

| Suffering | Struggling | Surviving | Thriving |

What I have been seeing in my work with organizational leaders is that most think they are surviving, but they are being too generous. Most leaders are either struggling or suffering. Only a very small percentage of leaders are thriving.

We cannot afford to have leaders who are, at best, merely surviving. **Rarely do we find a team that is in a better psychological state than its leader.** So, if a leader is simply surviving, it is likely their team is either struggling or suffering.

How then do we get leaders to go from suffering, struggling, or surviving to thriving?

One option is to wait around for the demands to decrease. But that is unlikely to happen.

A more assertive approach—and really the only option—would be to help leaders enhance their cognitive and emotional musculature. This would elevate their capacity to carry the weight of their challenging situations.

In the field of leadership development, our priority must be on elevating leaders' capacity to navigate the darkness of uncertainty, the chaos of complexity, and the winds of change without freaking out, burning out, or running out.

To achieve this goal, we must dramatically improve and accelerate our personal development as well as the development of other leaders within our sphere of influence. We must become more effective at elevating our load-carrying capacity to effectively operate amidst the change, pressure, uncertainty, and complexity that we face every day.

A New Form of Leadership Development

Unfortunately, traditional forms of developing leaders are not producing the leaders we need. These forms of development primarily focus on helping leaders gain more knowledge, skills, and abilities in a similar way that we download apps onto an iPad.

This form of development is well-intended, but it can only be helpful if the person's operating platform has the sophistication to use the apps that are downloaded.

What we are finding is that if leaders are simply equipped with new skills or knowledge—that is, we download new apps onto them—these apps are often more sophisticated than the operating platform they are being downloaded onto. When that is the case, the leaders are largely incapable of employing the new apps in the manner they were intended.

What we need is leadership development that focuses less on downloading new apps onto a leader and more on improving leaders' internal operating systems.

I have been a connoisseur of leadership development material for over twenty years, and I have been actively engaging in leadership development research and helping leaders develop for more than ten years. For the vast majority of this time, I have learned about and focused on the traditional forms of developing leaders—app downloads—because it is what has been primarily emphasized and focused on in the leadership domain.

It was not until about three years ago that I was introduced to a different stream of development thought that focuses less on downloading apps onto leaders via developing knowledge, skills, and abilities and more on upgrading leaders' internal operating systems by elevating their cognitive and emotional sophistication.

What surprised me is that this stream of development thought was not new. In fact, it has been researched for over fifty years. But the reason I had never been exposed to it is that it has been housed in a rather niche area of developmental psychology, and it has been overlooked by the leadership and management domains.

Yet, it seems to be something we have been itching for. Let me give you an example.

Jim Collins is a respected thought leader in the leadership space, and he is most well-known for his book, *Good to Great*. In this book, Collins identifies a certain type of leader that possesses the unique abilities to bring about transformational change in organizations. He identifies them as "Level 5 Leaders," the pinnacle of leadership. Collins's insights imply that if organizations want to transform and go from good to great, they need to either develop or select Level 5 Leaders.

Essentially, Collins is telling a similar story as I am. If organizations want to navigate more effectively now and into the future, they need to help their leaders elevate to a higher level of operation. They need leaders who have the capacity and operating platform required for navigating change, pressure, uncertainty, and complexity.

While Collins has long promoted the need for and the value of Level 5 Leaders, he has struggled to answer how one can develop into a Level 5 Leader. In an article published in the *Harvard Business Review*, Collins states, "We would love to be able to give you a list of steps for getting to Level 5—other than contracting cancer, going through a religious conversion, or getting different parents—but we have no solid research data that would support a credible list."

What Collins suggests is that to level up from a non-Level 5 Leader to a Level 5 Leader, we must transform ourselves.

I agree with his premise. Leveling up in our leadership is essential to leadership success, and it does require transformation, which may not be easy.

But what his statement indicates is that Collins is unaware of any development methodology that fosters the development of Level 5 Leaders.

What I have learned from a niche field within developmental psychology is there is a form of development that focuses on helping leaders level up—and do so without having to contract cancer, go through a religious conversion, or get new parents.

This form of development is called *vertical development.*

* * *

As you learn about vertical development, you will come to see that it is what leadership thought leaders have longed for because it is the key to developing any positive categorization of leadership.

While Collins promotes the need for Level 5 Leaders, Liz Wiseman in her book, *Multipliers,* calls for a shift in leadership from being a Diminisher to being a Multiplier. Likewise, Robert Greenleaf and Ken Blanchard are among many who advocate for the development of Servant Leaders.

There are also many other categorizations of higher-level leadership. These include conscious leadership, responsible leadership, future-ready leadership, and resilient leadership. But the thought leaders connected to these different categorizations have either not been clear about how to become such leaders, or they have primarily focused on the apps—knowledge and skills—leaders need to become such leaders.

Regardless of the type of leader that you want to be or the type of leaders you want to develop, **the only way that leaders can go from their current level of leadership to a higher level of leadership is with vertical development.**

Are you ready to better understand this key to leadership transformation and elevation?

CHAPTER TWO

THE DIFFERENCE BETWEEN HORIZONTAL AND VERTICAL DEVELOPMENT

Vertical Development Law #2
Different leaders may experience the exact same conditions, but if they are at different levels of vertical development, they will see the conditions differently, process the conditions differently, and respond differently to those same conditions.

If you are anything like me, computers play an increasingly pivotal role in your life. For me, my computer is a necessity. I do almost all of my work and communication through my computer, including teaching classes and conducting executive trainings. I do not anticipate the role computers play in our lives will diminish.

I believe the following is true about computers. See if you agree.

- More and more, computers are being called upon to fulfill increasingly sophisticated tasks.
- As a result, computers need to have broader and deeper capabilities than before.
- Computers we use every day (smartphones, tablets, laptops, or even cars, for example) are now required to possess capabilities that, historically, were only expected of high-end computers.

9

- This requires computer manufacturers to design highly adaptable computers with much greater capacity to successfully navigate a wide range of complex tasks and situations.

Knowing about rapid advances in technology and the need for your computer to be up-to-date, what do you do when you need to update your computer so that it can perform more complex functions? Do you download more programs and applications (or apps, in short), or do you upgrade the computer's operating system?

There are times when simply adding a new app would help, but if you want your computer to help you better perform the tasks you need to accomplish now, as well as into the future, the better approach is to upgrade the operating system.

Nowadays, upgrading your computer's operating system is so critical, your computer will regularly remind you to do so. The beauty of an upgraded operating system is that it more effectively coordinates all the functions of the software and hardware so your computer can perform at a higher level.

What does this have to do with leadership? you might wonder. Everything said about computers also pertains to leadership. See if you agree.

- More and more, leaders are being called upon to fulfill increasingly sophisticated tasks. This places greater and greater demands on leaders.
- As a result, leaders need to have broader and deeper capabilities than ever before.
- Leaders at all levels are required to possess capabilities that, historically, were only expected of the executive team, including broad conceptual capacity, divergent thinking, and creative problem-solving skills.
- This requires companies to develop highly adaptable leaders with elevated capacities to successfully navigate a wide range of complex tasks and situations.

Knowing of rapid advances in the world and the workplace, if you wanted to improve leaders' capacity to navigate their increasingly complex world, and you had to choose between giving leaders new programs by improving their knowledge or skills versus upgrading their operating systems by helping them think differently about the world and its challenges, which option would you choose?

What these options represent are two forms of leadership development: horizontal development and vertical development. I will describe each of them so you can decide which form of development is more effective.

HORIZONTAL VERSUS VERTICAL DEVELOPMENT

Horizontal Development

Horizontal development seeks to improve leaders' knowledge, skills, and abilities. It is similar to downloading a new program or app onto a computer, giving it greater functionality in some areas. The focus of horizontal development is to broaden leaders' functionality.

Horizontal development is by far the most common form of development. Think about any professional training you have received. It is more likely than not that those training events have been focused on providing you with new knowledge and skills so you can perform the tasks you could not do before.

While horizontal development helps you expand the things you can do, it does not improve the way you approach life's challenges.

* * *

One of the worst managers that I ever had was a man named George. The thing that grated me the most about George was the manner in which he thought. Not only was he a black-and-white thinker, but he also thought he was the smartest person in the room. According to George, he was always right, and his ideas were always better than everyone else's.

In team meetings, George was always giving commands; he rarely invited discussion. Whenever someone disagreed with him or provided a perspective different from his, George would get defensive, raise his voice, and try to beat the person's ideas down.

As you can imagine, under George's leadership, our work environment was not psychologically safe.

During George's tenure as manager, our organization conducted an employee engagement survey. While I am not sure what our engagement scores were, I do know that the organization had all the managers in the organization—including George—go through a series of workshops about engagement and psychological safety. These workshops took the standard horizontal development approach. They covered what engagement and psychological safety were, why they were important, and what managers could do to improve engagement and psychological safety.

Do you think this significantly changed how George thought and how he operated in meetings? Not really.

To give George some credit, shortly after the workshops he attempted to ask more questions rather than only give out directives. But this ended up becoming problematic for George. The more input and ideas he received from the team, the more defensive he got. This inevitably led to unnecessary and unhealthy conflict rather than a meeting of minds.

I saw this same approach to developing leaders and managers when I worked at Gallup, the employee engagement consulting company. On the back end of their employee engagement surveys, the trainings and resources Gallup provided to organizations primarily focused on telling managers what they needed to do to improve engagement, commonly in the form of boxes to check off.

This did not sit well with me as I have always believed that **effective leadership is not about *doing* the right things, it is about *being* someone that others want to follow.**

* * *

What I observed at Gallup, with George, and with most organizations is that the primary form of leadership development is horizontal development focused on improving leaders' knowledge and giving them a to-do list of things to accomplish. While this approach is not bad, it just does not result in the desired transformational change and improvement that organizations need.

Vertical Development

Thinking about George, are his shortcomings as a leader a knowledge and skills issue, or are they an operating system issue?

They are an operating system issue.

If George were ever going to improve as a leader, he would need to upgrade his internal operating system. He would need to alter some foundational needs, fears, and beliefs. Specifically, he would have to loosen his grip on his need to be right, his fear of being wrong, and his belief that there is only one right solution to every problem. Such transformation requires vertical development.

Rather than focusing on knowing more or doing more, vertical development focuses on helping leaders to *be* more. With vertical development, we are helping leaders rewire their minds and bodies so they can more effectively navigate conditions and situations that can otherwise be debilitating.

Vertical development is defined as elevating leaders' ability to make meaning of their world in more cognitively and emotionally sophisticated ways.

The basic notion involves understanding that one of the primary functions of our mind and body is to make meaning of the world around us. For example, at some point in our life, we did not know what a swastika was, and when we saw that symbol, it carried no meaning for us. Once we learned what a swastika represented, though, we began to make meaning of it in a specific way. Different people make meaning of swastikas in different ways, though. Long before it had a negative connection, it was and still is used as a Hindu and Buddhist symbol, called the gammadion cross. So, while most of us view this symbol negatively, others view it positively.

With every symbol we see and every situation we are in, our mind and body automatically, and largely nonconsciously absorbs information and makes meaning of it in unique ways. How exactly we make meaning of our world dictates the thoughts we have, the degree to which we learn, and the behaviors we engage in.

* * *

One of the biggest and most common issues I see with business executives is that they make meaning of or interpret failure as a signal that *they are* a failure. And when they see failure as a signal that they are a failure, they are reticent to try anything new, and they will instead stick to what they know and what has worked in the past. Unwilling to try new things and holding onto the past, the organizations they lead quickly fall behind the times.

This deep-seated and often unconscious fear of failure and looking bad is a self-protective mechanism that is surely justifiable. Who likes to fail or look bad? But while it may be safe, it is not very cognitively and emotionally sophisticated. And it limits how they think, learn, and behave as a leader.

* * *

When we understand that vertical development is about elevating leaders' ability to make meaning in cognitively and emotionally sophisticated ways, we are implying that across a population of people, people vary in how cognitively and emotionally sophisticated they are.

Do you have any guesses about what the distribution of cognitive and emotional sophistication looks like across a population?

It is not a bell curve distribution, where the majority of people are moderately cognitively and emotionally sophisticated. It is a Pareto distribution, which is similar to what wealth looks like in a population. Most people possess little cognitive and emotional sophistication, and as you go up the scale of cognitive and emotional sophistication, the fewer and fewer people you will find.

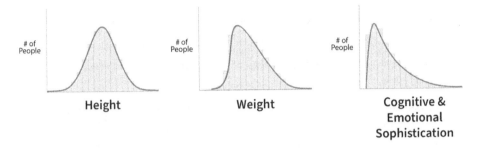

The purpose of vertical development is to help leaders move up the distribution into higher levels of cognitive and emotional sophistication, and as they do so, they will think, learn, and behave at higher levels. They will make better decisions and operate more effectively, especially under conditions of change, pressure, uncertainty, and complexity.

When leaders reach the highest levels of cognitive and emotional sophistication, they become a transformational force for good across their spheres of responsibility.

THE POWER OF COGNITIVE AND EMOTIONAL SOPHISTICATION: A COMPARISON OF MICROSOFT CEOS

The value and power of cognitive and emotional sophistication can be seen when comparing Steve Ballmer and Satya Nadella, the former and current CEOs of Microsoft.

In August 2012, the cover of *Vanity Fair* boldly proclaimed, "How Microsoft Lost Its Mojo." The preface to the article read:

> *Once upon a time, Microsoft dominated the tech industry: indeed, it was the wealthiest corporation in the world. But since 2000, as Apple, Google, and Facebook whizzed by, it has fallen flat in every arena it entered: ebooks, music, search, social networking, etc., etc. Talking to former and current Microsoft executives, Kurt Eichenwald*

finds the fingers pointing at CEO Steve Ballmer, Bill Gates's successor, as the man who led them astray.

When this article was released, Microsoft was valued at $250 billion, less than half of its peak valuation of $615 billion in 1999, and half the value of Apple, its primary competitor. Seventeen months after the *Vanity Fair* article, Steve Ballmer stepped down as CEO.

If you had bought $1,000 of Microsoft stock on the day Ballmer took over and sold it the day he stepped down, you would get $583.75.

Replacing Ballmer in 2014 was Satya Nadella. GeekWire suggested, "Satya Nadella gets to take on one of the most complex and difficult jobs in the business world—leading Microsoft through a period of massive change and challenges to its traditional businesses and trying to position the company to identify and capitalize on the next big things in technology, whatever they turn out to be."

Nadella was quickly able to prove that he had what it takes to succeed as a leader in "one of the most complex and difficult jobs." Within three years of Nadella stepping in, Microsoft had doubled its value. Since then, Microsoft has experienced exponential growth, with its market capitalization climbing to over $2 trillion. Satya Nadella has Microsoft operating on a whole other level.

If you had bought $1,000 of Microsoft stock on the date that Satya Nadella took over as CEO, and sold it on May 1, 2022, you would get $7,709.

* * *

If we were to liken Steve Ballmer and Satya Nadella to computers, here is how they would compare. I believe it is safe to say that Ballmer and Nadella largely have the same base programs on their computer. They have a similar background, similar knowledge of the company and of the industry, and they have similar skills. From a horizontal perspective, they both seemed to have the requisite programs to operate as CEO.

They differ significantly, though, in the cognitive and emotional sophistication of their internal operating systems. Let me demonstrate.

When Ballmer took the stage in front of Microsoft employees, he generally did so like a rock star. (You can see clips of this on YouTube.) Music would be blaring, and he would jump and dance around on stage in a sweat-drenched shirt, yelling, "I! Love! This! Company!"

Those inside and outside of Microsoft called this his "monkey-boy dance." These on-stage antics characterized Ballmer's charisma, brashness, and passion.

In contrast, when Nadella took the stage for the first time as CEO, he presented a purpose-fueled challenge, stating, "The business of ours is an exciting business. And one of the core things we've got to realize is that this business doesn't really respect tradition. What it respects is innovation on a go-forward basis. So, it's really our collective challenge that we now need to make Microsoft thrive in a mobile-first and a cloud-first world."

This epitomizes how Nadella communicates with Microsoft employees. He does not seek to superficially hype them up. Instead, he takes the more cognitively and emotionally sophisticated approach of centering Microsoft employees around a common and meaningful purpose and then seeks to inspire and elevate those employees to fulfill that purpose.

> ## Vertical Development: An Extreme Example
>
> I once heard big-wave surfer Mark Mathews give a speech titled, "The Other Side of Fear." He told the audience that to prepare his mind and body to survive a crash while riding a big wave, he hired a scuba diver to wrestle with him forty feet underwater, even to the point of blacking out. Doing so helped Mark expand his capacity to stay calm, cool, and collected in even the most dangerous circumstances.
>
> Fortunately, we do not need to expose ourselves to threatening situations to develop vertically. A big part of vertical development, though, is connecting with and getting to the other side of our fears.

In fact, an emphasis on possessing a clear purpose is another huge differentiator between Ballmer and Nadella.

Ballmer was not "a mission and purpose guy." During his tenure as CEO, Microsoft still pursued the mission that Bill Gates had coined, that is, to put a computer on every desk and in every home. Almost fourteen years after taking over from Gates, Balmer tried to promote a new mission to guide Microsoft.

On July 11, 2013, he sent an email to all employees with the title, "One Microsoft." In that message, Ballmer called for a sharpened strategy focused on "creating a family of devices and services for individuals and businesses that empower people around the globe at home, at work, and on the go, for the activities they value most." Six months later, having had no time to implement this mission, Ballmer stepped down as CEO.

Nadella, on the other hand, knew that having a clear mission and purpose is essential. To discern their next mission and purpose, Nadella devoted much of his first year to listening and learning from Microsoft employees at every level and every part of the company. He wrote, "Listening was the most important thing I accomplished each day because it would build the foundation of my leadership for years to come."

At the company's global sales conference in July 2015, a year after Nadella took over the leadership of Microsoft, he presented a new mission statement that would guide Microsoft into the future: "To empower every person and every organization on the planet to achieve more."

To this day, this is a strong guiding mission and north star for all Microsoft employees.

Both Ballmer and Nadella possessed the knowledge and skills to construct and promote a clear purpose. But Ballmer operated with an internal operating system that was wired for different priorities, like fighting their competitors.

The difference between Ballmer and Nadella's approach toward Microsoft's market rivals— Apple, Google, and Amazon—is equally astounding.

Ballmer's internal operating system is wired to compete. In one of his more quotable moments, he stated, "In many dimensions [my children are] as poorly behaved as many other children. But at least on this dimension, I've got my kids brainwashed: You don't use Google, and you don't use an iPod."

At a corporate event, when Ballmer spotted an employee taking a picture of him using an iPhone, he snatched the device from the employee, put it on the ground, and pretended to stomp on it before walking away.

Nadella's internal operating system, on the other hand, is not wired to compete. It is wired to collaborate. In one of his first public presentations as the face of Microsoft, he reached into his suit jacket and pulled out an iPhone. There was an audible gasp.

"This is a pretty unique iPhone," he told the attendees. "I like to call it the iPhone Pro because it's got all the Microsoft software and applications on it."

In his book, *Hit Refresh*, Nadella writes, "Today, one of my top priorities is to make sure that our billion customers, no matter which phone or platform they choose to use, have their needs met so that we continue to grow. To do that, sometimes we have to bury the hatchet with old rivals, pursue surprising new partnerships, and revive longstanding relationships."

Finally, when it comes to the cultural tone that each CEO set for Microsoft, one of the biggest cultural blunders of Ballmer's tenure was the implementation of stacked rankings as part of employees' performance reviews.

This approach forced managers to rank their employees from best to worst, and the employees' bonuses were determined by their rankings. While Ballmer had hoped this approach would allow the company to invest more heavily in the people and positions deemed most critical to the success of the organization, it wreaked havoc on Microsoft's culture as employees competed with each other for positive rankings. This destroyed the culture at Microsoft.

Ballmer's ranking system also caused employees to self-protect. They felt like they always needed to look good, that they could not make mistakes, and that they had to have all the answers. It formally and socially incentivized close-mindedness and inhibited innovation.

When Nadella became CEO, he recognized that Microsoft's culture was in triage and declared that the *C* in CEO stands for "curator of culture," establishing it as his number one priority. To improve Microsoft's culture, Nadella focused on helping employees develop a growth mindset as the primary means of shifting Microsoft's culture to one where, in an effort to learn and grow, it became OK to fail or make mistakes.

Essentially, what the vertically developed Nadella was doing—and is still doing—is encouraging and supporting the vertical development of Microsoft employees. He does not want employees to feel the need to be know-it-alls; he wants them to be learn-it-alls. Nadella intuitively knows that if employees can vertically elevate, Microsoft will become more of the innovative company they have always aspired to be.

While this cultural shift has been foundational to Microsoft's success during Nadella's tenure, it took a leader with a certain level of cognitive and emotional sophistication to pull it off.

* * *

The difference between Ballmer and Nadella is not about a difference in programs. What sets apart Nadella from his predecessor is his ability to make meaning of his world in more cognitively and emotionally sophisticated ways.

It seems clear that Ballmer's internal operating system is programmed to stand out, as this seemed to be his focus both personally and for Microsoft. He walked on stage like a rock star. He did not care much about a company mission. He was driven to stand out from Microsoft's competitors. And he implemented a performance management system designed to identify employees who stood out.

Nadella's internal operating system seems programmed to contribute and elevate. When he walks onto a stage, he does so with the intention to elevate employees with clarity and purpose. After listening to the employees of Microsoft, he developed a mission that has inspired them to operate at a higher level. He recognizes that Microsoft will go further and higher if they nurture strategic partnerships with competitors. And his primary emphasis as CEO has been on raising the culture of Microsoft, believing that as the culture is elevated, the success of the company will follow suit.

While Ballmer possessed the knowledge and skills to be every bit as successful as Nadella, his approach to leadership was not sophisticated enough for the company he was leading and the circumstances in which it was navigating.

Under Ballmer's leadership, Microsoft exerted much effort but got nowhere. But under Nadella's leadership, Microsoft has propelled forward and continues to grow at an exponential pace.

That is the difference vertical development can make.

USING VERTICAL DEVELOPMENT TO ELEVATE OUR IMPACT

As I promote the ideas of vertical development and the notion of internal operating systems being either *more* cognitively and emotionally sophisticated or *less* so, I occasionally get feedback that the analogy with computers feels too sterile and talking about "cognitive and emotional sophistication" seems snooty. Honestly, this feedback is not wrong, but at the moment, it is the best and clearest way I have found to bring vertical development to life.

Something you will realize as we go through this book is that vertical development and cognitive and emotional sophistication is anything but sterile and snooty. When you look at the most vertically developed leaders—people like Satya Nadella, Nelson Mandela, Martin Luther King Jr., Alan Mulally, and others—they are anything but sterile and snooty.

The most vertically developed leaders and people are dynamic, complex, warm, and humble. They have an uncanny capacity to bring both the mind and the heart to the situations they encounter. They are the ones who breathe life and positive energy into the people and the world around them.

They are able to do this because they have rewired their minds to seek out and fulfill higher-ordered needs and live higher-ordered values. This does not make them perfect or better than other people; it makes them more capable of having a healing and transforming impact on the world around them.

The great news is that we can all upgrade our internal operating systems. We can elevate our abilities to take on and successfully navigate increasingly complex tasks with greater speed, effectiveness, agility, creativity, and mastery. We can all develop vertically to have more of a Nadella-like impact compared to a Steve Ballmer-like impact.

Elevating your being through vertical development and becoming an elevated leader is what this book is about.

CHAPTER THREE

THE ORIGINS OF VERTICAL DEVELOPMENT

Vertical Development Law #3

As leaders' altitude of vertical development rises, they become more conscious of the dynamics of their world. They can see further, see more clearly, see more details, and see more interdependently.

When I first learned about vertical development, I was surprised to learn the concepts around this rare type of leadership development have been around for about fifty years; though, these ideas have not always been labeled as "vertical development." In fact, this label did not come into use until about ten years ago, when organizational psychologists started introducing these concepts into the leadership and management space.

Part of the reason why these ideas have not become more mainstream is that for most of the last fifty years, they have been relatively hidden in a niche field of developmental psychology.

EARLY DEVELOPMENTAL PSYCHOLOGY

As a field of study, developmental psychology has been around for almost 140 years. For the first eighty years, developmental psychologists largely neglected the development of adults, and the focus was almost solely on childhood development. This is largely because as children progress through childhood and into adulthood, their development is easily observable. Developmental psychologists initially neglected the development of adults because it was largely assumed that cognitive and emotional maturation essentially stopped after people entered adulthood.

As a result, if you were to take a college developmental psychology class, much of the class would be focused on childhood development stages. Depending upon the textbook used, the number of these stages focused on would range from three to seven.

The general assumption was that while adults can always learn new things or develop new skills, their cognitive and emotional maturity essentially stops progressing once they enter adulthood.

Even today, this assumption is widely held. This is part of the reason why development efforts focus significantly more on individuals' knowledge and skills than on their cognitive and emotional maturity.

ADULT DEVELOPMENT PSYCHOLOGY

About sixty years ago, though, a few developmental psychologists began pushing against conventional wisdom. They wondered if it was possible for adults to develop cognitively and emotionally during adulthood, and if so, does their development progress through stages in a fashion similar to how children develop.

Taking this perspective, research pioneers, including Robert Kegan, Jane Loevinger, and Lawrence Kohlberg, began studying adult cognitive and emotional maturation in the form of conscious, ego, and moral development. Each of these perspectives has since been refined and, at times, merged. This can be seen in the work of some modern-day adult development psychologists, including Terri O'Fallon, Suzanne Cook-Greuter, William Torbert, Antoinette Braks, and others.

Across the research of all these individuals, there is consensus around three primary findings:

1. Adults can develop and mature cognitively and emotionally. This form of development is what we now refer to as vertical development.
2. Generally, there are three base stages of adult vertical development.
3. While it is possible for adults to develop vertically through different stages, relatively few actually do develop vertically.

Adults Can Vertically Develop

What developmental psychologists have realized is that *all* people, regardless of age, possess a sense-making system, something I have been referring to as our "internal operating system." This sense-making system consists of principles, beliefs, thinking patterns, and assumptions that govern how we make meaning of and experience life.

Through childhood experiences, this system routinely shifts and adapts to help the individual most successfully navigate their environment. What plays out is that no two people have the same internal operating system. They make meaning of their world in different ways, carry different thought patterns, and possess different assumptions.

I saw this recently while camping with my extended family. My children were playing by a mountain stream with one of their older cousins. My children approached a large log spanning the stream and were about to cross when their cousin called out, "I wouldn't cross if I were you. You could fall."

My children ignored him and crossed to the other side of the stream. This cousin approached the log, hesitantly stepped onto it, and took a shuffle or two heading toward the other side before giving up and going back to where he started.

After observing several instances where this cousin was fearful and hesitant about doing things that most children are readily willing to do, I asked him why he was being so cautious. "I have PTSD from our camping trip last year," he told me.

His response surprised me. I did not expect an eleven-year-old to know what post-traumatic stress disorder was, plus I was unaware of anything bad happening to him the year before. He told me about an accident where an ATV he was riding on had turned onto its side. Although he was physically unharmed, it was clear that he was emotionally harmed.

Comparing this cousin to my children, he had a formative experience that altered his sense-making system. He now saw our camping area and activities as being full of hazards that should be avoided, while my children viewed the same camping area and activities as adventures that should be explored.

Both perspectives are valid. But because of the difference in their sense-making systems, these cousins think and operate differently. Comparing my children to their cousin, it is reasonable to believe that if they maintain their sense-making systems, my children would probably be more willing to attempt new things. In the process, they will learn more, develop more and broader skills, and probably have more scrapes and bruises.

* * *

You and I have likewise had formative childhood experiences that have affected our sense-making, or internal operating systems. As we entered into adulthood, we continued to rely upon our internal operating system, which was the byproduct of our upbringing.

We would do well to ask ourselves, "Is the internal operating system that allowed me to successfully navigate my childhood the same internal operating system that will allow me to be effective as an adult, in a career, in a marriage, as a parent, and as a leader?"

The likely answer is no.

What adult development researchers have found is that nearly all people enter adulthood with a sense-making system that is simple rather than complex. It is neither very mature nor sophisticated.

Through vertical development, you can improve your body's sense-making or internal operating system in adulthood. Vertical development researchers have found that when you develop vertically and continue to do so, you follow a predictable pattern.

This pattern represents the stages of vertical development.

There are Different Stages of Vertical Development

Across my study of vertical development, I have observed that the prominent psychologists studying adult development as well as the thought leaders in this field have all developed their own frameworks for what they see as the stages of vertical development.

The basic notion behind these vertical development frameworks is that when people develop vertically, they elevate and improve their internal operating systems through a sequence of stages. As they progress from stage to stage, their meaning-making, beliefs, thinking patterns, and assumptions change from being less simple to more complex, and from being less cognitively and emotionally sophisticated to more cognitively and emotionally sophisticated, allowing them to navigate their world more effectively and successfully.

Not all vertical development thought leaders agree on the number of vertical development stages. One framework had twelve stages, another six stages, and another three stages. But what almost all vertical development thought leaders agree upon is that there are three base or primary stages of vertical development. My focus in the remaining first half of this book is on describing each of these three base stages and helping you see what they look like in life. For now, I will hold off on elaborating.

Not All Adults Do Vertically Develop

Adult development researchers have found that while adults *can* develop vertically, most do not. So, what percentage of adults progress beyond the first stage of vertical development?

Based on his vertical development assessment, Robert Kegan has the most data to answer this question. One of his samples focused on the general adult population, while another sample focused exclusively on executives, primarily chief executive officers.

In his sample of the general adult population, Kegan found that 64 percent of adults operate primarily in the first stage of vertical development. In other words, most adults never improve their internal operating system beyond the level they reached in childhood.

Kegan's research further found that 35 percent of adults develop into the second stage of vertical development, while a meager 1 percent developed into the highest and most sophisticated stage of vertical development.

In his sample of CEOs, he found that only 7 percent of executives operated in the first stage of vertical development, 85 percent in the second stage, while 8 percent primarily operated in the highest and most sophisticated stage of vertical development.

KNOWLEDGE IS POWER

Until a couple of years ago, I had never heard about vertical development, let alone its various stages. My ignorance limited me in two ways.

My first limitation was that when I focused on either developing myself or others, I was primarily focused on horizontal development techniques and efforts. I would focus primarily on improving my knowledge, skills, and habits. I did not even consider trying to alter my meaning-making system.

For example, in the past, as I wanted to become more of a Level 5 Leader, a Multiplier, and a Servant Leader, I devoted a substantial amount of time learning about these types of leaders. While learning about these different forms of leadership helped me identify some things that I could do differently than before, this learning did not significantly alter my sense-making system and, therefore, did not transform the way I viewed and processed life events.

Some of my coaching clients have expressed a similar sentiment. After I introduced them to vertical development, they admitted that their focus had been on gaining degrees and certifications, believing that the additional knowledge and skills associated with such certifications would help them become a more effective person and leader. But no matter how many certifications they had, their thinking did not change, nor did they feel like a better person.

The second limitation was that I had previously no way to measure my level of vertical development. But once I learned about the three stages of vertical development, I could better assess my vertical altitude. Though I was disappointed to realize I was not as sophisticated as I thought I was, this new lens has helped me to become more self-aware regarding my current state of development, and it has given me greater clarity about where I need to go.

* * *

I have since worked with thousands of leaders on vertical development and have found that not even 1 percent of leaders know about vertical development, and even fewer can identify the stages of vertical development.

Not surprisingly, leaders think about development in terms of horizontal development. Many believe they are fully developed, that they have all the knowledge and skills necessary for their role as leaders. But what they cannot see is that, even if they do possess a great amount of knowledge and skills, their current level of cognitive and emotional sophistication is likely preventing them from utilizing their knowledge and skills in the most effective way.

THE JOURNEY AHEAD

Now that you have seen the difference vertical development can make in the success of a leader, we will focus on the following in the remainder of this book:

- Identifying the stages of vertical development.
- Understanding what level you are currently primarily operating at.
- Developing vertically so that you make meaning of your world in more cognitively and emotionally sophisticated ways and elevate as a leader.

I hope and expect that by reading the remainder of this book, you will experience vertical development. And as you improve how you see and make meaning of your world, you will become a more elevated version of yourself.

Before we go into our next chapter, pause and take a vertical development assessment. It is only fifteen questions.

It has been designed to help you identify your current stage of development. You can take this assessment by going to the following link:

www.ryangottfredson.com/vertical-development-assessment

I have found that individuals respond to the questions more authentically if they take the assessment before learning about the vertical development stages. So, if you want to get the most accurate results, I suggest taking the assessment before you continue to Chapter Four.

CHAPTER FOUR

INTRODUCING THE THREE LEVELS OF VERTICAL DEVELOPMENT

Vertical Development Law #4

Leaders at a higher level of vertical development can see why someone at a lower level of vertical development operates the way they do. But leaders at a lower level of vertical development have a hard time seeing why someone at a higher level of vertical development operates the way they do.

Brandon Sanderson is the author of *The Stormlight Archive*, a fantasy series that tracks the vertical development of one of the main characters, Kaladin.

In the fantasy world of *The Stormlight Archive*, individuals can develop vertically in a step-like fashion. In order to step up from one vertical development level to the next, individuals must overcome personal challenges and, in the process, gain new understanding and insights that allow them to speak and make an oath, called an "ideal." Once that ideal has been spoken, characters are endowed with greater abilities and greater responsibility to lead, serve, and protect humanity.

When we first meet Kaladin, he is a downtrodden slave. But over time, he goes through experiences that allow him to utter the increasingly sophisticated ideals. In doing so, he is able to level up in both his cognitive and emotional sophistication as well as his physical abilities. This not only allows him to gain his freedom; it also allows him to become a great warrior and an increasingly better person and leader.

To illustrate the character's personal growth and development, author Brandon Sanderson places Kaladin in very similar circumstances over different stages of his development. In doing so, the reader can compare and contrast how Kaladin evolves in the ways that he thinks and operates as a result of his increasing levels of cognitive and emotional sophistication.

At the beginning of the series, Kaladin is living under the first ideal: "Life before death, strength before weakness, journey before destination." It is an ideal that is somewhat noble, but also self-protecting. At one point, a slaver is upset with Kaladin and rears back to strike him. Given the ideal that he lives under, Kaladin instinctively cowers to preserve his own life. The idea of fighting back did not occur to him because that would mean putting his life at risk.

Later, Kaladin becomes a leader of a slave crew, and he takes on the more sophisticated second ideal: "I will protect those who cannot protect themselves." In a similar circumstance as before, a slaver is upset at Kaladin and rears back to strike him. This time, being under this second ideal, Kaladin instinctively fights back as a way to protect those under his stewardship. The idea of cowering did not seem like a viable option as doing so would have put his crew at risk.

Fast-forward in the series and Kaladin rises to the third and more sophisticated ideal: "I will take responsibility for what I have done. If I must fall, I will rise each time a better man." By rising to this ideal, Kaladin increased his powers and abilities and became a Knight Radiant, a rare breed of people. As a Knight Radiant, Kaladin has gained special powers that make him suited to be a protector of the kingdom he is a part of.

At one juncture in the series, an enemy army has captured the city where Kaladin is living. The enemy knows a Knight Radiant is hiding within the city but does not know who it is. Kaladin attempts to stay unknown so he can continue serving and helping his people, now living under the watchful eye of the enemy.

At one point, the enemy closes in on Kaladin's whereabouts, and an enemy soldier comes upon him. Believing Kaladin to be a regular person, the soldier does not recognize him as the Knight Radiant.

After Kaladin resists the direction of the soldier, the soldier rears back to hit him. This time, Kaladin does not instinctually cower or fight back. Instead, now able to see and appreciate the world with greater sophistication and complexity, he instantaneously weighs the pros and cons of either option. He makes the intentional decision to cower to help ensure he is not discovered as the Knight Radiant they are looking for so he can go on serving and helping his people.

* * *

Across these three different moments, Kaladin was presented with essentially the same situation. But in each situation, he was at a different level of vertical development and, thus, responded to those situations with a different level of cognitive and emotional sophistication.

Under the first ideal, he was focused on self-protection and instinctively cowered.

Under the second ideal, he was focused on helping his team progress and instinctively fought.

Under the third ideal, being more conscious and intentional, he embraced the complexity of the situation and made the calculated decision to put his physical well-being on the line to provide the best long-term help to the people he cared about and served.

What vertical development researchers have found is that *if* adults develop vertically to the highest vertical development levels, they generally proceed in their development in a three-step fashion similar to that demonstrated by Kaladin.

LEVELS OF VERTICAL DEVELOPMENT

There are three base levels of vertical development. I call them Mind 1.0, Mind 2.0, and Mind 3.0. I use the term *mind* because that is where our internal operating system resides and where vertical development occurs. And I use the language "1.0," "2.0," and "3.0" because each level represents a different internal operating system that is programmed to fulfill specific needs and quell specific fears.

In the upcoming chapters, I will reveal the specific programming associated with the three mind levels and the characteristics that manifest at each level. What is fascinating to me about these mind levels is that psychologists have found that the operating system at each mind level dictates 90 percent of our actions—including our thinking, feeling, judging, and acting—primarily at a nonconscious level.

What this means is that at whatever level we are at, we will think, feel, judge, and act in a manner aligned with that level's programming. The manner in which we think, feel, judge, and act will come so naturally and feel so right that we will not question it, and we will remain at that level, believing we are operating in the best way possible.

But as we view these three mind levels from an objective perspective, two things should occur. First, you should get a sense of why most people primarily operate in Mind 1.0, why most executives and leaders primarily operate in Mind 2.0, and why reaching Mind 3.0 is necessary for truly effective leadership.

Second, and more importantly, you will also be able to gauge your current level of vertical altitude as well as that of people you work and live with. Gaining clarity regarding your vertical altitude and that of others, you will deepen your self-awareness and awaken to how developing vertically will allow you to become a more positive influence within your sphere of influence. And as someone who cares about growing others, you will come to more fully understand and appreciate just how essential vertical development is in leadership development.

Ready to dive in? As you go through these three mind levels, ask yourself, "At what level do I spend the majority of my time?" Then see if your results from the vertical development assessment align with your self-assessment.

CHAPTER FIVE

MIND 1.0: SELF-PRESERVATION MODE

Vertical Development Law #5
The greater a leader's vertical development altitude, the more capable they are at dealing with change, pressure, uncertainty, and complexity.

Remember Blockbuster Video? Back in the day, Blockbuster captured 25 percent of the video rental business in the United States. Perhaps you were one of their nearly twenty million members.

During the early part of his tenure as Blockbuster CEO, John Antioco saw Blockbuster revenues rise from roughly $3.5 billion to $5 billion annually. In 1999, Antioco had led the company through an initial public offering, raising more than $450 million in cash. Blockbuster was flush with cash and in a solid position in the marketplace.

The next year, a struggling start-up called Netflix came knocking. Their business model was to let people rent DVDs online and then receive them in the mail. Financially, two-year-old Netflix was not in a great position. But what they did have going for them was a vision of a future world where people would consume videos digitally instead of through DVDs.

Reed Hastings and Barry McCarthy—the CEO and CFO of Netflix—were granted a meeting with Antioco and his team. Hastings pointed out that Blockbuster was in a great position in their marketplace of brick-and-mortar DVD rental stores, but Netflix held a strong position in the online space.

Hastings suggested that Antioco buy Netflix. Hastings and company would run Blockbuster's online business. Antioco objected, suggesting that online businesses were not sustainable. "The dot-com hysteria is completely overblown," he said. Curious, Antioco asked the Netflix duo for the dollar figure.

Hastings asked for $50 million.

McCarthy describes seeing Antioco's earnest facial expression change to a slight smile. McCarthy interpreted this as Antioco struggling not to laugh. The Netflix team was sent packing.

By 2011, Blockbuster was out of business, largely because they never committed to an online presence. Their demise will forever be linked to Antioco.

Meanwhile, Netflix is now the largest streaming service in the world, valued at $230 billion.

* * *

There is one word that has been commonly used in the media to describe large companies that have flamed out. The word is *complacent*. If you were to ask Antioco about that fateful meeting, he would likely adamantly deny being complacent. And so would the CEOs of Circuit City, Toys 'R' Us, Kodak, and Sears, all large companies that flamed out.

"Circuit City became complacent," *Time Magazine* reported, "a fatal mistake in the fiercely competitive and fast-evolving retail-electronics industry."

Commenting about Toys 'R' Us, Wharton Business said, "Company leaders became complacent after years of sitting at the top of the toy-store game, and they did nothing to improve stores, adapt to technology or tackle competition head-on."

An article in *Forbes* used the same word when describing Kodak. "The organization overflowed with complacency. I saw it, maybe in the late

1980s. Kodak was failing to keep up even before the digital revolution when Fuji started doing a better job with the old technology, the roll-film business. With the complacency so rock-solid, and no one at the top even devoting their priorities toward turning that problem into a huge urgency around a huge opportunity, of course they went nowhere."

The same goes for *Investor's Business Daily*'s description of the company that was once headquartered in the tallest building in the world. "Sears became complacent and failed to respond to the ever-changing retail market."

I do not think any of the leaders of these companies thought they were being complacent. I imagine they all thought they were working their tails off to try to help their companies succeed.

What was the problem then? In each of these instances, what was going on is that the leaders were operating with an internal operating system that was programmed to fulfill the needs to feel safe and comfortable and like they belong, the primary needs of Mind 1.0. When leaders operate at this mind level, their drive and decision-making focused on safety and comfort shows up as complacency.

We should all be able to relate to Mind 1.0 programming. Most of us stepped from childhood into adulthood with Mind 1.0 programming. And most people, 64 percent of all adults to be exact, stay stuck operating primarily in Mind 1.0.

Thus, as I describe the characteristics of Mind 1.0, consider the parts of you that still reside at this level and how these parts may lead others to see you as being complacent.

FOUNDATIONAL NEEDS AND FEARS OF MIND 1.0

An apt label for this level is self-preservation mode. When we function in Mind 1.0, our internal operating system is primarily programmed to ensure three needs are met: our safety, comfort, and belonging. In Mind 1.0, fulfilling these needs feels natural, right, and justified. In fact, anything that does not feel safe, comfortable, or does not lead to belonging feels wrong.

Conversely, in Mind 1.0, we fear being unsafe, uncomfortable, and alone. This causes us to think in the following ways:

- Why would I embrace ambiguity and complexity? Ambiguity and complexity make me feel stressed out, anxious, and unproductive.
- Why should I deal with the hassles of taking charge if someone else is willing to do it?
- Why would I want to rock the boat? It will only cause problems.
- Why go through the hassle of figuring out the answers myself or coming up with direction when others can do it for me?
- Why would I ever want to stand out from my tribe? It is better to fit in.

The behaviors that push against us in Mind 1.0—embracing ambiguity and complexity, taking charge, rocking the boat, figuring out the answers, coming up with a direction, and standing out—are not intrinsically bad. In fact, as we will discuss later, a lot of good can come from doing these things. However, the Mind 1.0 operating system sees these as threats to our safety, comfort, and belonging, and they are, therefore, perceived as being bad.

Just as a thermostat senses temperature changes and turns on the heater when it gets too cold, a Mind 1.0 operating system is sensitive to threats to our safety, comfort, and belonging. It sets off alarm bells throughout the body that loudly screech, "Regulate! Regulate! Regulate!" Once that happens, all bodily resources are directed toward ensuring they return to a place of safety, comfort, and belonging.

For many, the fear of being unsafe, uncomfortable, and alone becomes a strong driver throughout their lives, keeping them stuck in Mind 1.0.

One way I summarize Mind 1.0 is by saying we are programmed to *stand in*. By *standing in*, I mean being as close to the center of the group as possible. It is a place where we feel the safest, most comfortable, and like we belong. *Fitting in* or *blending in* does not quite communicate that, so I am coining a new usage of *stand in*.

* * *

Remember Kaladin? Under the first ideal (representative of operating in Mind 1.0), he was unable to see beyond ensuring his own safety, comfort, and belonging. That is why he instinctively cowered when threatened by a slaver. He neither thought about the team he was a part of, nor did there seem to be a reason why he should consider the pros and cons of a response other than cowering. Kaladin sensed immediate danger, and his internal operating system served to protect him.

THE THREE HALLMARKS OF MIND 1.0

There are three hallmarks of those who operate in Mind 1.0. The first is that we are prone to join groups and become devoted group members. These groups can be family, friends, social groups, religious groups, political groups, professional associations, recreational teams, and more. We seek to join groups because we see them as a source to help us secure our need for safety, comfort, and belonging, and they help us quell our fears of being unsafe, uncomfortable, and alone.

In Mind 1.0, when we join a group and that group provides safety, comfort, and belonging, we will identify strongly with that group. It even becomes a part of who we are. This identification has both pros and cons. The pros are that we can receive the benefits of safety, comfort, and belonging among other tangential benefits like friendship, respect, and comradery. But on the downside, we can be overprotective of the group, and if someone were to criticize the group—even if the criticism is accurate and justifiable—we would likely respond in a closed-minded and defensive manner.

The second hallmark of being in Mind 1.0 is that we become dependent thinkers. In Mind 1.0, we do not want to take charge or make decisions. That can feel unsafe and uncomfortable and may lead to us not belonging. Thus, we give up our power and independence in exchange for the group fulfilling our needs and quelling our fears. We essentially say to the group: "I have no interest in taking charge or making decisions. That seems unsafe and uncomfortable. But if you will give me direction and tell me what to do, I will gladly do those things provided that you keep me safe, comfortable, and feeling like I belong." This willingness to give up our power and independence and the reluctance toward making our own decisions makes us dependent thinkers.

An example of where we can slip into becoming dependent thinkers are around political elections. Some of us essentially operate in a way where we tell our political party, "I don't care to research the candidates or the issues on the ballot. Just tell me how to vote, and I will vote that way." But this form of dependent thinking does not only apply to politics.

Pay attention, and you will see it at work where someone might figuratively say, "I don't want to be in charge, but if you will tell me what to do and give me a paycheck, I will do it." Or in religious groups, where someone might figuratively say, "I don't want to figure out what beliefs, morals, and values I should espouse. I'll let the religious leaders do that for me as long as I feel safe, comfortable, and like I belong to this congregation."

The third hallmark of Mind 1.0 is that we become short-term oriented. Our biggest priority in Mind 1.0 is feeling safe, comfortable, and like we belong—*in the moment*. We go from situation to situation with a certain amount of caution and anxiety about the degree to which we will be safe, comfortable, and feel like we belong.

With this short-term focus, we have little ability or desire to think about the future. This is especially pronounced when we feel unsafe, uncomfortable, and like we do not belong, for when those needs are not being met, we can think of little else.

ADDITIONAL CHARACTERISTICS OF MIND 1.0 LEADERS

When we understand that those in Mind 1.0 are programmed to be safe, comfortable, and belong, and are therefore devoted group members, dependent thinkers, and short-term oriented, we can predict how we will operate across different situations.

The table below outlines the characteristics and common behaviors of those who operate in Mind 1.0.

Characteristics and Common Behaviors When We Operate in Mind 1.0	
To stay safe, we . . .	· Become unwilling to take risks. · Are cautious, slow, and passive. · Like to stick to a clear plan, and we have a hard time thinking outside the box and being agile, creative, and innovative. · Promote culture for the purpose of helping people feel safe and comfortable. · Have a narrow window of tolerance. · Get defensive when we receive constructive criticism.
To stay comfortable, we . . .	· Are unwilling to take on learning zone challenges, challenges beyond what we have done before, will stretch our knowledge and abilities, and are generally not attainable in a single attempt. · Are inclined to resist change. · Prefer to stick with what has worked in the past and are reluctant to embrace new methods. · Are problem-avoiders. · Prefer to be sympathetic as opposed to empathetic. · Avoid conflict. · Avoid asking for feedback.
To belong, we . . .	· Are people pleasers. · Prioritize doing things that will help us better fit in with our social groups. · See vulnerability as something that will lead to ostracism. · Prioritize looking good and avoiding challenges because, should we fail, we believe others will reject us. · Are sensitive about our relationships and social status.

As dependent thinkers devoted to our groups, we . . .	· Are rule followers.
	· Are reluctant to lead.
	· Avoid taking initiative and responsibility.
	· Are closed-minded to ideas from outside our group.
	· Are narrow-minded.
	· Have weak egos.
	· Are meek.
	· Value people who are similar to us.
	· Think of those in our in-group as being more valuable and important than those in our out-group.
	· Avoid questions.
	· Struggle with complexity.
	· Tend to be polarized thinkers.
	· Get defensive when our beliefs are questioned.
Being short-term oriented, we . . .	· Are impulsive.
	· Only worry about the moment.
	· Believe others should be very sensitive to our emotions.
	· Do not like to think ahead and make plans because those plans may get in the way of doing what will help us to feel safe, comfortable, and like we belong in that moment.

THE DARK SIDE OF MIND 1.0

While Mind 1.0 programming helps ensure that we feel safer, more comfortable, and like we belong—all good things, in themselves—this programming has two large unintended negative side effects.

Mind 1.0 Limits Our Ability to Connect with Others

The core focus of Mind 1.0 programming is on protecting ourselves. We are programmed to put our need for safety, comfort, and belonging ahead of others' needs, whatever they might be. Our safety takes precedence over the safety of others. Our comfort takes precedence over the comfort of others. And our belonging takes precedence over the belonging of others.

A byproduct of this self-protective programming is a lack of concern for others. Being so focused on our own safety, comfort, and belonging, we exhibit a dampened ability to be sensitive and aware of the safety, comfort, and belonging of others, particularly those that fall outside of the groups that we are a part of, especially when we are not feeling safe, comfortable, or like we belong.

For those of us who are at a higher level within Mind 1.0, this focus can extend to our group. In that case, the safety, comfort, and belonging of our group members take precedence over the safety, comfort, and belonging of other groups and their members.

But when we are in Mind 1.0, our self-protection places a barrier between us and others. In my life, I have seen this show up as a lack of sensitivity toward others, especially in how I used to view homeless people.

* * *

For much of my adult life, I viewed homeless people asking for assistance as a threat to my safety and comfort. As such, I was quick to be condescending toward them, commonly thinking, *Why would I give you my hard-earned money? Why don't you put forth more effort to find a job?*

In Mind 1.0, I was unable to acknowledge their humanity. I could not find it within me to consider all they may have gone through in life to end up on the streets. And I certainly did not consider their lack of safety, comfort, and belonging.

In all, when we are in Mind 1.0, our self-protection places a barrier between us and others, especially when we are not feeling safe, comfortable, or like we belong.

Mind 1.0 Limits Our Ability to Reach Our Potential

The second negative side effect of Mind 1.0 is portrayed well in the Disney movie, *Moana*. Moana is the strong-willed daughter of a chief of a Polynesian village located on a small island in the South Pacific.

Moana feels called to the ocean, but her father, Tui, is constantly discouraging her from going out into the ocean, citing how much danger there is beyond the reef. In the movie, Tui sings, "Where You Are" to Moana.

In this song, Tui uses strong Mind 1.0 programming within the lyrics. The language is all about staying on the island, where it is safe, comfortable, and where belonging can be had—all justifiable. But the effect of such language is that it keeps the island's people, particularly Moana, from experiencing a broader world. Spoiler alert: Moana goes on to explore the world beyond the reef, just as her ancestors had done.

When we are concerned about our safety, comfort, and belonging, we become unwilling to try new things and get outside of our comfort zones. By staying on our islands, in our safe zones, we become insular, closed to ideas and philosophies that exist beyond our groups.

Not being willing to go beyond our own "reefs," we ultimately live below our potential.

* * *

When I work with executives and business leaders on their vertical development, I have them work through a vertical development coaching exercise. For 90 percent of these clients, we have identified Mind 1.0 programming to be a foundational obstacle to their leadership effectiveness. This programming most commonly shows up in fears of looking bad, failing, or not being of value, all self-protective fears that feel right, normal, and justifiable.

When my clients discover these deep, generally unconscious fears, they are able to see how these fears prevent them from operating more effectively as a leader. For example, one leader with a fear of looking bad was holding herself back from being a more active participant in executive meetings, one leader with a fear of failing was micromanaging his employees, and one leader with a fear of not being of value was taking credit for the work of his subordinates. Clearly, these leaders' Mind 1.0 operating systems were holding them back from being the positive influences they desired to be.

Every time I have these conversations with my clients, I am reminded of when my children learned how to navigate the monkey bars. They would take a brave step and grab onto the first bar, letting their feet dangle. But no sooner were they in this position than they realized that if they wanted to get across the monkey bars, they were going to have to let go with one hand to grab the next bar. They also knew if they let go of the bar, there was a chance they might fall and hurt themselves.

I watched more than once as my children would simply hang there, holding tightly to the first bar. They would quickly give up on their goal to get to the other side and instead prioritized their safety and comfort. This is no different than the biggest challenge we adults face in our journeys of vertical development.

If we want to move to a higher level, accomplish our goals, and have a greater positive impact, we have to loosen our grip on our primal need for safety, comfort, and belonging. We have to strengthen our resolve to reach our goals of becoming elevated leaders and that resolve has to be stronger than our need for safety, comfort, and belonging.

When we care more about our safety, comfort, and belonging, we will never let go of the bar. But when we care more about our goal, we become willing to let go with one hand and reach to the next bar, a necessity for crossing the monkey bars.

MIND 1.0 LEADERS

While adults stuck in Mind 1.0 generally avoid taking on leadership positions, research shows that 64 percent of all adults and 7 percent of all executives operate primarily in Mind 1.0. That means that within most organizations, more than half of the staff and some of the leaders are stuck in Mind 1.0.

When we find ourselves in leadership positions as men and women with a Mind 1.0 internal operating system, we often lead from one of two extremes.

Mind 1.0 Leaders Tend to Be People Pleasers

As Mind 1.0 leaders, we are consistently seeking the acceptance of those we work with. We want to be seen as a friend and peer of those we lead. As such, we avoid evaluating our employees, often neglect giving feedback or coaching for improvement, and avoid difficult conversations and even making decisions, all out of fear that we might disappoint others, damage our relationships, and not belong.

Mind 1.0 Leaders Tend to Be Controlling

By being in control, we can better ensure our safety and comfort. Mind 1.0 leaders hate problems, ambiguity, and complexity, and being in strict control is a way to avoid such things. In fact, in this state, we are generally more focused on avoiding problems and difficulties than we are on reaching goals. As such, we commonly find our teams busy but not making progress. We resist change; we push against new ideas, and we end up getting stuck in the past.

An example of a Mind 1.0 leader is Henry Ford, the founder of Ford Motor Company. Ford is fascinating because, in some ways, he was incredibly inventive and innovative. Earlier in his career, he developed the automated assembly line. But he was also extremely controlling.

One of several examples of Ford's need for safety and comfort was when he introduced the Model T into the world. In many ways, the Model T changed the world. It was a smashing success. Interestingly, it took Ford twenty years before he produced a car different from the Model T. Henry Ford was unwilling to make changes, to do something different than what he did with the 1908 Model T. He refused to upgrade the cars the Ford Motor Company was producing.

During those twenty years, other car manufacturers were developing better vehicles while Ford's market share declined. On more than one occasion, Henry Ford's need to stay where it was safe and comfortable nearly killed his company.

MIND 1.0 SUMMARY

Mind 1.0: Also known as self-preservation mode

Stats: 64 percent of adults operate primarily in Mind 1.0, and 7 percent of executives find themselves at this level

Mind 1.0 Needs

- Safety
- Comfort
- Belonging

Mind 1.0 Fears

- Lack of safety
- Discomfort
- Lack of belonging

The Dark Side of Mind 1.0

- Limited ability to connect with others
- Limited ability to reach our potential

Mind 1.0 Leaders

- Tend to be people pleasers
- Tend to be controlling

* * *

Were you able to recognize yourself in some of these traits? Whether you currently operate primarily in Mind 1.0 or not, we have all spent significant time at this level. It is a natural part of our human experience.

In his emails and app messages called "Notes from the Universe," Mike Dooley wrote, "When the fear of 'things staying the same' exceeds the fear of 'failure,' stuff happens." And Mind 2.0 is where we move past our fears of being unsafe, uncomfortable, and not belonging, and stuff begins to happen. It is where we are going next. While Mind 2.0 has its own significant limitations, it is an upgrade from Mind 1.0.

CHAPTER SIX

MIND 2.0: SELF-FOCUSED REWARD MODE

Vertical Development Law #6
When leaders have risen in their vertical elevation and traverse previous terrain, they will see it differently, interpret it differently, and likely navigate it differently.

As we upgrade our internal operating system from Mind 1.0 to Mind 2.0, we loosen our grip on our need for safety, comfort, and belonging, and we grab onto the need for standing out, advancing, and getting ahead.

FOUNDATIONAL NEEDS AND FEARS OF MIND 2.0

In fact, at the Mind 2.0 level, we become willing to be unsafe, uncomfortable, and not belong so we can stand out, advance, and get ahead. At the same time, we tend to keep score of how much we are standing out, advancing, and getting ahead by accumulating pleasures, wins, gains, results, recognition, praise, popularity, power, privileges, and successes.

As we take on the Mind 2.0 needs, we also take on new fears. These include standing in, being stuck, and falling behind.

The shift from Mind 1.0 to Mind 2.0 is a shift from self-preservation mode to self-focused reward mode. We go from wanting to stand in to wanting to stand out.

In addition to the shift in needs and fears, as we progress from Mind 1.0 to Mind 2.0, the way we think and process the world around us also changes.

As a Mind 2.0 person might push to stand out, advance, and get ahead, a Mind 1.0 person will wonder, "Why would you want to do that? Standing out is dangerous, it will feel uncomfortable, and it may prevent you from fitting in."

Meanwhile, as a Mind 1.0 person works hard to be safe, be comfortable, and fit in, the Mind 2.0 person will wonder, "Why would we ever want to play it safe? Standing in will only slow you down and make you redundant, and you won't be recognized as being someone of value."

It is this phenomenon that explains why Kaladin was willing to cower to a slaver at one time and fight a slaver at another time. At different times in his development, he possessed very different internal operating systems.

As a reminder, 35 percent of all adults and 85 percent of all executives operate primarily in Mind 2.0.

THE THREE HALLMARKS OF MIND 2.0

When we operate in Mind 2.0, we are not dependent thinkers like we were in Mind 1.0. Instead, we become independent thinkers. We become willing to push against the beliefs and norms of our groups and develop our own belief systems. No longer are we confined by the "shoulds" and "oughts" of the group we belong to; we come up with our own rules to guide us.

While some of our beliefs may still be aligned with our group's beliefs, we are now standing on our own two feet as opposed to leaning on the group around us. By standing on our own two feet, we are separating our identity from the group we have been a part of.

Generally, becoming independent is courageous. It means we are getting outside of our comfort zones and acknowledging that, in developing our independent beliefs, we may no longer fit in or belong. Hence, to make this shift to independence, we generally have to feel quite strongly about our beliefs. A common side effect of this is that when we function in Mind 2.0, we can become close-minded.

The next hallmark of being in Mind 2.0 is that we become more self-directed. In Mind 1.0, we want to stay in a safe and comfortable location, and we are fine being told what to do. But once we shift into Mind 2.0, we care more about making self-determined progress. We become focused on reaching goals and setting milestones. Reaching those goals and hitting those milestones means progress and advancement for which we can be recognized.

Also, when we function in Mind 2.0, we recognize that there are many people stuck in Mind 1.0 who are willing to give up their power and independence for safety, comfort, and belonging. Recognizing this, we are willing to step into leadership roles and use the power and independence that those in Mind 1.0 are willing to give up to help us accomplish our needs for standing out, advancing, and getting ahead. This is a primary reason why 85 percent of executives operate in Mind 2.0.

The third hallmark of being in Mind 2.0 is that we become short-term oriented. But our short-term orientation is different than when we lived in Mind 1.0. In Mind 1.0, our short-term goals were focused on being safe, comfortable, and belonging. In Mind 2.0, our short-term goals are focused on the degree to which we are standing out, advancing, and getting ahead.

A Mind 2.0 CEO is commonly more focused on short-term objectives, like quarterly and annual revenue, profits, and stock price rather than on purpose, culture, and innovation, which will impact revenue, profits, and stock price five or ten years down the road. When we function in Mind 2.0, we are sensitive to what we can do *right now* to make progress and accomplish the next milestone to satisfy our needs for progress and advancement.

* * *

One way I regularly see this short-term orientation in my work with executives, business owners, and managers is when I offer trainings on the importance of investing in culture. It is common to have leaders at these events ask, "Why should we spend our time, energy, and resources focusing on culture when we can spend them on things that more directly generate revenue, like sales, marketing, and gaining market share?"

In asking this question, they are exposing their Mind 2.0 internal operating system. They are focused on what will make them look good in the short run, and they struggle to see the necessity of a positive and intentional culture for long-term success.

ADDITIONAL CHARACTERISTICS OF MIND 2.0 LEADERS

When we understand that those in Mind 2.0 are programmed to stand out, advance, and get ahead, and are therefore independent, self-directed achievers, with a short-term orientation, we can predict how they will operate across different situations.

The table below outlines the characteristics and common behaviors of those who operate in Mind 2.0.

Characteristics and Common Behaviors When We Operate in Mind 2.0	
To stand out and be recognized, we . . .	· Prioritize performance (e.g., profits, revenues, hours worked) and are generally quite anxious about our performance or the performance of our groups.
	· Will only take on challenges we know we can be successful at.
	· Have a small window of tolerance for failure because if we fail, we believe our failure is a signal that we will not be valued or recognized.
	· Are generally quite competitive.
	· Loosen our need to be accepted by social groups.
	· See vulnerability as a sign of weakness.

To advance and get ahead, we . . .	· Are eager and energetic. · Like to go fast. · Are willing to take risks. · Are willing to embrace change if it will help us be successful in the short run. · Avoid problems and failures. · Possess low care and compassion for others, particularly if they are slowing down our advancement in some way.
Being independent thinkers and self-directed, we . . .	· Emphasize cognition over emotion. · Are commonly narrow-minded. · Are commonly closed-minded to ideas that contradict our beliefs. · Have clear goals and are willing to ruffle feathers to accomplish our goals. · Want to be in positions of leadership. · Are commonly commanding.
Being short-term oriented, we . . .	· Struggle to be agile and adjust systems because doing so may disrupt our short-term performance and success. · Do not strongly value culture because it takes time and resources away from accomplishing our short-term goals. · Will see conflict and negotiation as opportunities to compete and win, and we are significantly more likely to approach these situations than those in Mind 1.0, who are more inclined to avoid these situations.

THE DARK SIDE OF MIND 2.0

There can be a huge upside to being an initiative-taker with an outcome orientation focused on winning. Such qualities can drive people to accomplish great things and have a huge positive impact on the world.

But a strong focus on standing out, advancing, and getting ahead can have two large unintended negative side effects.

Mind 2.0 Drives Us to be Self-Focused

When our internal operating system is programmed to stand out, advance, and get ahead, we are not focused on others or even on a bigger purpose. Instead, we become focused only on ourselves. We are wired to chase what is best for us in terms of standing out, advancing, and getting ahead.

Intertwined with Mind 2.0 programming is a certain degree of ego (sometimes a lot of ego), arrogance, and competitiveness. While these can be strong forces for great energy and action, they generally cause collateral damage to the people around us.

Often, what this looks like in business leaders is an attitude of profit over people. As mentioned previously, when we operate with a Mind 2.0 internal operating system, we become willing to take the power and independence of these Mind 1.0 others to help us fulfill our need for standing out, advancing, and getting ahead, and we commonly neglect to provide the safety, comfort, and belonging that the Mind 1.0 people expect and need. In essence, in Mind 2.0, we are prone to step on others to get what we want.

* * *

I wish the list of CEOs who have been criticized for this type of behavior was shorter. The list includes—but is not limited to—Jack Welch (GE), Steve Ballmer (Microsoft), Lee Iacocca (Chrysler), Al Dunlap (Sunbeam), Kenneth Lay (Enron), Jeffrey Skilling (Enron), John Stumpf (Wells Fargo), Travis Kalanick (Uber), Carly Fiorina (Hewlett Packard), Stan O'Neal (Merrill Lynch), Angelo Mozilo (Countrywide Financial), and David Solomon (Goldman Sachs).

These are all Mind 2.0 leaders who have, at times, made a lot of progress, but they were not value creators, and they ultimately wreaked havoc on their organizations.

Mind 2.0 Drives Us to Be Finite-Minded

Mind 2.0 programming can also commonly lead to us being finite-minded. The concepts of being finite-minded versus infinite-minded have been popularized in *The Infinite Game* by Simon Sinek.

When someone is finite-minded, they see their world as a finite game that is played by known players. The game has fixed rules and an agreed-upon objective that, when reached, ends the game. Players are focused on beating their competition, as is the case with most sports.

When someone is infinite-minded, though, they see their world as an infinite game played by unknown players. The game has changing rules and no conclusion. When someone views the world as an infinite game, their objective is to continue playing the game in the best way possible. There is no winning. With this mentality, the players do not focus on beating out the competition, they focus on delivering and adding value to their stakeholders. They see that as the best way to stay in the game.

A great example that Sinek gives is of Apple and Microsoft during the Steve Ballmer era. At Microsoft's education summit, Sinek observed that most speakers devoted a good portion of their time talking about how to beat Apple. But at Apple's education summit, he found, "One hundred percent of the presenters spent one hundred percent of their time talking about how Apple was trying to help teachers teach and help students learn."

Microsoft was playing the finite game and was focused on competing, while Apple was playing the infinite game and focused on adding value.

When we operate with a Mind 2.0 worldview, we are programmed to play the finite game. This may have some short-term benefits but generally has severe long-term negative repercussions.

MIND 2.0 LEADERS

As pointed out, research has shown that 85 percent of all executives operate primarily in Mind 2.0. This likely means the majority of leaders and managers below the executive level also make meaning of their world from a Mind 2.0 stance, but probably less than 85 percent. This should not be surprising because those in Mind 1.0 generally prefer to avoid managerial and leadership roles, while those in Mind 2.0 see managerial and leadership roles as a way to stand out, advance, and get ahead.

In working with Mind 2.0 leaders, I have found they have two major tendencies.

Mind 2.0 Leaders Tend to Be Progress Makers, Not Value Creators

In Chapter Two, we contrasted Steve Ballmer with Satya Nadella. By now, it should be clear that Steve Ballmer seemed to operate on a Mind 2.0 internal operating system. Recall that he put on a show when he went on stage; he did not seem concerned about a long-term mission; he was very competitive, and he instituted a stacked-ranked performance management system that severely damaged Microsoft's culture. Ballmer wanted to stand out, win, and look good. He was also short-term and finite-minded.

Steve Ballmer was well-intended. He meant well. He did a lot of good things. He worked tirelessly, and he made a lot of progress. But he was never able to elevate the organization to a level higher than when he took over as CEO.

Another leader to consider here is Jack Welch, the former CEO of General Electric. He is a leader that was able to dramatically grow his organization. During his near-twenty-year tenure as CEO of General Electric, he saw GE go from being worth $14 billion to being worth $400 billion and a stock price that increased by 4,000 percent. He became wildly respected and famous for this growth.

In hindsight, though, we have great cause to be skeptical of his leadership. If we look under the surface, his success is a prime example of Mind

2.0 in action. It now seems clear that he played a finite game focused on making progress and hitting short-term shareholder expectations as opposed to playing the infinite game focused on creating value.

His nickname was "Neutron Jack," which is in reference to him shutting businesses and clearing staff who failed to meet expected returns. Specifically, Welch implemented the "rank and yank" policy that led to GE laying off 10 percent of managers every year, which included more than 170,000 employees in his first ten years.

One of Welch's most popular books is simply titled, *Winning*. That title has Mind 2.0 written all over it.

Unfortunately, GE is currently a shell of what it used to be because Welch made decisions that would benefit the stock price in the short run but cripple the company in the long run.

Mind 2.0 Leaders Tend to Hinder Agility

Most executives and leaders I work with are in Mind 2.0. When I first meet them, they almost always believe they are doing a really good job, yet their organizations are stagnant, slow, and not at all agile.

As I work with these leaders, I explain vertical development to them and present the three mind levels. I invite them to consider, "Is it me? Am I the one—despite my best intentions and best efforts—who is holding back the organization because I am operating with a Mind 2.0 internal operating system?"

This questioning is very difficult for them to stomach. My clients have risen into their leadership positions largely because their strong Mind 2.0 drive to stand out, advance, and get ahead has allowed them to demonstrate hard work, determination, and success. For them, their Mind 2.0 operating system is a proven formula for success. And then I come along and essentially tell them they can level up and that doing so requires a complete paradigm shift. This is not an easy pill for them to swallow.

Of all the executives I have coached, about half of them get defensive and dismissive as we try to identify the mind level that they operate from. When they discover their self-protectiveness and finite-mindedness, I often hear objections, such as, "I have to operate this way because . . ."

My clients give a very justifiable reason for their Mind 2.0 thinking and actions. One executive was willing to admit that he was a bit of a micromanager. He justified this by saying, "I *have* to operate this way because my staff is young and inexperienced. The only way that I can get things done and get things done *right* is to be really hands-on with them."

To avoid defensiveness from arising too quickly with my clients, I have found it helpful to ask them this question before I present anything related to vertical development: "Is a company more likely to positively transform with a leadership team that has been in place for five years or a new leadership team?"

Most of them choose the latter, saying, "A new leadership team."

"Why is that?" I ask them. Common responses include:

- "A new team cares less about or is unaware of the politics that have built up over time."
- "A new team is less emotionally connected to past decisions and projects and is more willing to let go of the old and embrace the new."
- "A new team can be more demanding of change in the employees below them."

These are all valid points. But it leads me to ask another question: "What would it take for the incumbent leadership team to overcome current politics, be willing to let go of the old, and be more demanding of change?"

While my clients initially struggle to answer this question, we are generally able to come to the answer that in order for an incumbent leadership team to change deeply rooted thinking, processes, and politics, vertical development of the team members must occur. The leadership team needs to level up and change the paradigms from which they have been operating.

It is at that point I address the fact that for leaders to develop vertically and change their paradigms, they need to admit to themselves and others that they have room to grow, and they have to work at developing vertically. Vertical development has to be a priority for them.

Unfortunately, it is common for executive teams *not* to prioritize vertical development as they are too busy fighting the fires that have sprung up due to their Mind 2.0 leadership.

* * *

What I am describing here connects back to what we discussed in Chapter One. Leaders commonly run on a leadership deficit. The complexity of their situations exceed their current vertical altitude. It is not simply that they are too big for their britches. Instead, their britches are too big for them.

This dilemma was aptly described in *American Icon*, a book about the transformation of the Ford Motor Company under the leadership of Alan Mulally. What set the stage for Mulally to come in as CEO and Ford's ultimate transformation was Bill Ford's recognition that the britches he was wearing were too big for him and then doing something about it to elevate the organization.

Bill Ford became Ford's chairman and CEO in 2001. During the first year of his tenure, Ford performed reasonably well. But from 2002 to 2006, Ford Motor Company was bleeding money. It was set to lose $12.7 billion in 2006. Under these circumstances, Bill Ford admitted, "No single individual can run this company effectively under the current circumstances. I need help."

Bill Ford essentially admitted that the situation he was facing surpassed his vertical altitude. This is when they brought in a Mind 3.0 leader, Alan Mulally, who transformed Ford into one of the most respected brands in the world. More about Mulally in the next chapter, though.

MIND 2.0 SUMMARY

Mind 2.0: Also known as the self-focused reward mode
Stats: 35 percent of adults operate primarily in Mind 2.0, and 85 percent of executives find themselves at this level
Mind 2.0 Needs

- Standing out
- Advancing
- Getting ahead

Mind 2.0 Fears

- Standing in
- Feeling stuck
- Falling behind

The Dark Side of Mind 2.0

- Drives us to be self-focused
- Drives us to be finite-minded

Mind 2.0 Leaders

- Tend to be progress makers, not value creators
- Tend to hinder agility

* * *

All told, those in Mind 2.0 have what we would classify as a moderate amount of cognitive and emotional sophistication. They have moved on from the Mind 1.0 needs to be safe, comfortable, and belong and have embraced the Mind 2.0 needs to stand out, advance, and get ahead. In making this transition, they have also shifted from being a dependent thinker to an independent thinker. While there are some benefits to Mind 2.0 programming, the dark side of Mind 2.0 can be quite severe.

If we truly want to have a positive and transforming influence within our spheres of responsibility, we have got to level up to a Mind 3.0 operating system.

That is what we will focus on next.

CHAPTER SEVEN

MIND 3.0: CONTRIBUTION MODE

Vertical Development Law #7

Leaders are able to operate at any altitude level they have traversed in the past, but they cannot operate at an altitude level that is higher than what they have traversed so far.

W here you see transformational and sustainable change in an organization, you will find a leader operating in Mind 3.0. We have seen this in the leadership of Satya Nadella, who took a stagnant Microsoft in 2014 and has lead the company to the point where Microsoft's stock price is more than seven times greater than it was when he took over as CEO.

And, as hinted at in the previous chapter, the same happened at the Ford Motor Company in 2006. Ford was set to lose $12.7 billion when Alan Mulally was brought in as CEO. Not only did Mulally bring Ford back to profitability, but he also set them up for long-term success. Since Mulally took the reins, Ford has consistently been at or near the top of lists that feature the best corporate brands and the most respected companies in the world. And in 2009, Ford was the only American automaker that did not need bailout funds following the economic crisis of the year before.

Admittedly, Ford has not been performing as well since Mulally stepped down. From my study of the situation, though, it seems that

Mulally laid a foundation for long-term success, but subsequent leaders have not been able to capitalize on it.

In the same year Ford brought on Mulally, Disney bought Pixar Animation Studios. At the time, Disney Animation Studios was struggling to produce blockbuster movies. They had recently produced the widely criticized, *Lilo & Stitch*, and they had a number of recently produced flops to their name, including *Treasure Planet* and *Home on the Range*.

Disney Animation Studios had lost its life and its vitality. So, Disney made Pixar's president, Ed Catmull, the president of Disney Animation. Under Catmull's leadership, Disney went on to create blockbusters like *Frozen* and *Frozen II*, *Toy Story 3* and *Toy Story 4*, *Zootopia*, and *Coco*—all among the top twenty for highest grossing animated movies of all time.

The reason why Satya Nadella, Alan Mulally, and Ed Catmull were able to create transformational and sustainable change is because they operated with a Mind 3.0 internal operating system.

In fact, among all of the Mind 3.0 business leaders I have studied, I believe these men are among the best examples. From studying their leadership, I have come to believe that a prerequisite for any transformational and sustainable change in an organization is to have a leader operating in Mind 3.0.

FOUNDATIONAL NEEDS AND FEARS OF MIND 3.0

You may remember that, in Mind 1.0, our internal operating system is programmed to stand in. Our priorities and drive revolve around our safety, comfort, and belonging.

In Mind 2.0, our internal operating system is programmed to stand out. Our priorities and drive revolve around standing out, advancing, and getting ahead.

At these lower levels of development, our programming is self-focused. If any of these needs are threatened, we make decisions and take actions to ensure we either stand in or stand out. Generally, our response to any threats to these Mind 1.0 and Mind 2.0 needs is self-protective and defensive. In the moment, it may feel good and even right to ensure our needs are met, but the protectiveness and defensiveness tend to cause collateral damage to the organizations, groups, and people we lead.

In Mind 3.0, though, our internal operating system turns from being self-focused to being outward-focused. When we operate in Mind 3.0, our needs are to contribute, add value, and lift others. At this level, we are not only willing to put our safety, comfort, and belonging on the line, but we are also willing to put our standing out, advancing, and getting ahead on the line in order to contribute, add value, and lift others.

People who operate at this level are rare. You may remember that only 1 percent of adults, in general, and 8 percent of executives operate at this level.

The Mind 3.0 internal operating system also comes with fears. But these fears are not necessarily negative, as they are not self-protective, like the Mind 1.0 or Mind 2.0 fears associated with not standing in or not standing out. The Mind 3.0 fears involve the fears of not being of value, taking from, or limiting others.

* * *

A great example of a Mind 3.0 leader is Martin Luther King Jr. Based upon King's writing, speeches, and actions during the Civil Rights Movement, his programming seemed to be focused on contributing and adding value to a higher purpose focused on lifting and elevating others.

King did not operate in Mind 1.0. Not that he was unconcerned about his safety, comfort, and belonging, but he was willing to sacrifice these things to fulfill his higher purpose.

Nor did he lead from Mind 2.0. Not that he did not do things to stand out, but when he stood out, it was to fulfill his higher purpose of equal rights for all races—not to fulfill a need to be recognized.

THE THREE HALLMARKS OF MIND 3.0

The first hallmark of those in Mind 3.0 are that they are emotionally centered and balanced. Back in Mind 1.0 and Mind 2.0 mode, we see things like failing, being wrong, having problems, and getting passed up as being threats to us standing in or standing out. Thus, when we fail, are wrong, have problems, or get passed up, we get thrown outside of our window of tolerance, and we become defensive and resistant. We feel like we need to save face.

When we operate in Mind 3.0 and are emotionally centered and balanced, we have a wider window of tolerance for failing, being wrong, having problems, and getting passed up. In fact, rather than get defensive and resistant when these things occur, we are able to harness the power of these challenges.

In doing so, we see failure as an opportunity to learn and grow, being wrong as a step toward finding truth, having problems as a signal of progress, and getting passed up as an opportunity to grow. This wider window of tolerance allows us to be more centered and balanced in instances that rattle most others.

As an example, consider the breadth of Satya Nadella's tolerance when a core project had a massive failure and problem. In March 2016, Microsoft's Future Social Experiences Labs unveiled an artificial intelligence chatbot called Tay. Tay was designed to learn and get smarter the more people chatted with it. Unfortunately, the release did not go as planned.

Shortly after the launch, people started tweeting the bot with racist and misogynistic remarks. Being a learning device based upon its inputs, Tay began repeating these sentiments back to users. It was garbage in, garbage out. Within twenty-four hours, the bot tweeted 96,000 times, becoming increasingly vile.

This was bad publicity for Microsoft. Commenting on this launch, one Twitter user observed, "'Tay' went from 'humans are super cool' to full nazi in <24 hrs and I'm not at all concerned about the future of AI."

How do you think Steve Ballmer would have responded to this situation? I believe he would have come down harshly on the project leaders. Satya Nadella was undeterred, though. He sent a message to Tay's creators, telling them, "Keep pushing, and know that I am with you."

Nadella's window of tolerance for failure and problems was so wide that when they occurred, he did not feel threatened, nor did he get emotionally or cognitively hijacked. Instead, Nadella remained balanced and centered, which allowed him to respond in a way that fostered greater commitment and future innovation.

The second hallmark of operating in Mind 3.0 is that we become interdependent thinkers as opposed to dependent or independent thinkers. This means that we can see and hold multiple and complex perspectives simultaneously.

When we see the world from Mind 1.0 and Mind 2.0, we dislike complexity and generally rush to simplify our world so we can better stand in or stand out. But when we function from Mind 3.0, we recognize we can make the best decisions and take the best action when we see the richness and the details of our world. Thus, we are quick to gather information and slow to judge.

Take any social or political issue, and you will find people who quickly rush to one side of the aisle or the other and generally take a rather strong stance there. But when we function from Mind 3.0, we are comfortable sitting right in the middle of the aisle, as this is the place where we can best see the issues at hand and weigh the pros and cons of the differing perspectives. This is not to say that we never take a stand. But before we ever take a stand, we, as Mind 3.0 leaders, want to make sure we understand the complexities of the issue.

The third hallmark of operating from Mind 3.0 is that we become long-term oriented. As you may recall, when we were stuck in Mind 1.0 and Mind 2.0, we were focused on standing in or standing out in the short term. But as we grow in our cognitive and emotional sophistication, broaden our windows of tolerance for potential threats to our safety or advancement, and become interdependent thinkers, we become less concerned about the short term, and we become primarily focused on contributing and elevating over the long term.

Our programming in Mind 1.0 and Mind 2.0 is to neglect or even sacrifice the long term in favor of the short term. Our programming in

Mind 3.0 does not weigh the short term too heavily and is even willing to sacrifice it if necessary for long-term performance.

By being balanced and centered, an interdependent thinker, and long-term oriented, we effectively operate as a wise sage. We are free from the self-protective short-term need for standing in or standing out, have the ability to wade in complexity, and are able to see the forest for the trees. This allows us to operate from a place of wisdom and sound judgment. In doing so, we are able to be calm in the midst of a storm.

ADDITIONAL CHARACTERISTICS OF MIND 3.0

When we understand that, when operating in Mind 3.0, we are programmed to contribute, add value, and lift others, and are balanced, interdependent thinkers with a long-term orientation, we can predict how we will generally operate across different situations. Here is a list of various characteristics and common behaviors of those in Mind 3.0.

Characteristics and Common Behaviors When We Operate in Mind 3.0	
To contribute and add value, we . . .	· Prioritize lifting and serving others; we understand that the more we add value to others, the more value we get in return. · Are purpose-focused. · Create a shared and meaningful vision. · See vulnerability as a sign of strength. · Seek to collaborate.
To lift others, we . . .	· Do not seek after certain positions. Instead, we seek after opportunities to have a positive influence. · Are empathetic and care about the emotions of others. · Value the unique differences and characteristics of others.

Being interdependent thinkers who embrace complexity, we . . .	· Are humble. · Are always asking questions. · Are deeply self-aware. · Are open-minded to ideas that are from outside of our group and/or contradict our beliefs. · Emphasize both the heart and the mind. · Consider the perspective of all stakeholders.
Being balanced and centered with a wide window of tolerance, we . . .	· Get excited about learning zone challenges. · Recognize that, while we may not be successful on our first try, if we can persist, we will be able to conquer the challenge. · Recognize that change is a constant, and we welcome it. · Have an absent ego.
Being long-term oriented, we . . .	· Are willing to take risks to set up a better future position. · Approach challenges that may lead to failure because we believe that failure is a stepping stone to success. · Value culture as a long-term strategy for lifting others and long-term success.

THE BRIGHT SIDE OF MIND 3.0

By now, you know that people with a Mind 3.0 internal operating systems are rare. Their high-level meaning-making systems do not have a self-protective dark side, like in Mind 1.0 or Mind 2.0. Instead, this level is marked by meaningful and uplifting bright sides. In fact, an apt description of Mind 3.0 people is that they cast a positive light on nearly all the situations they encounter, and their light is both a beacon and direction for others.

I have found there to be eight bright points to the Mind 3.0 internal operating system, and these set Mind 3.0 people apart from others.

1. Mind 3.0 People Are Emotionally Intelligent

One of my pet peeves is that emotional intelligence is predominantly treated as a horizontal development topic. There seem to be near endless trainings about what emotionally intelligent people do differently. But emotional intelligence is a vertical development topic, as it is deeply rooted in our internal operating system. As a result, a horizontal development approach to emotional intelligence can, at best, only be incrementally helpful.

Most emotional intelligence frameworks identify four components of emotional intelligence—the first two being inward-focused and the last two being outward-focused components. The inward-focused components are being aware of our own emotions and being able to regulate them effectively. The outward-focused components are being aware of others' emotions and being able to respond to them effectively.

Later, we will look at the connection between vertical development and emotional intelligence at a neurological level. For now, suffice it to say, when we operate from Mind 1.0 or Mind 2.0, we possess a narrow window of tolerance for perceived threats to our ability to stand in or stand out, and we struggle to regulate our emotions effectively, particularly under stress. Further, while in Mind 1.0 and Mind 2.0, because we are so wrapped up in either our standing in or standing out, we are limited in our capacity to be aware of others' emotions and respond to them effectively. In fact, in Mind 1.0 and Mind 2.0, we tend to make self-serving decisions that benefit ourselves but are insensitive and detrimental to others.

When we elevate to Mind 3.0, we expand our window of tolerance and become less self-protective. This puts us in a cognitive and emotional state that allows us to better connect with and regulate our emotions. Further, being more balanced internally, we are better able to be sensitive to and respond to others' emotions with empathy.

2. Mind 3.0 People Have a Good Relationship with Time

In Mind 1.0 or Mind 2.0, we are wired to be anxious about both the past and the future. We worry about whether we will stand in or stand out in and wonder if we have done anything that is hindering our ability to stand in or stand out. Worrying about our future and agonizing about we have done in the past, we struggle to be present and in the moment.

But in Mind 3.0, we are centered and balanced. When we are not concerned about whether we are standing in or standing out, we have a greater ability to be fully present. This ability to be present allows us to bring the version of ourselves each situation requires.

Also, when we operate in Mind 3.0, we can see, appreciate, and value both the short term and the long term. This is something we have difficulty doing in Mind 1.0 and Mind 2.0. On these lower rungs of development, we generally struggle to take our eyes off the short term and think about the long term.

Something I often notice is that when in Mind 1.0, we struggle to make plans for the future, even on a week-to-week basis. We also tend to scoff at using time-management tools and planners. When we are in Mind 1.0, planning and structure feel limiting, and they prevent us from feeling able to secure our safety, comfort, and belonging. In Mind 2.0, however, we are more inclined to use time-management tools and planners, but we do so primarily to make sure we are checking everything off our list so we can hit our short-term goals.

In Mind 3.0, we have the ability to step back and see the bigger picture. We can look ahead and connect the present to the future. This allows us to make the best decisions in the present for everyone's future.

When Mind 3.0 people use time-management tools and planners, we use them not simply as to-do lists, but as strategic tools that help us prioritize our time so we can place proper emphasis on those things that will set us up for success in the long term.

3. Mind 3.0 People Are Systems Thinkers

When we operate in Mind 2.0 and are short-term-focused progress makers, we are almost solely concerned with measurable outcomes and making sure we exceed any expectations related to achieving those outcomes.

With this focus and only being independent thinkers, we, as Mind 2.0 leaders, have a hard time seeing and valuing the systems and processes that go into long-term outcomes. In Mind 3.0, though, being more long-term oriented and interdependent thinkers who can sit in complexity, we prioritize the systems and processes that go into the outcomes over the outcomes. We "work the angles," knowing that getting the systems and processes right will lead to long-term effectiveness and success. When we work the angles, we take our eyes off the outcomes we desire and focus instead on the drivers of those outcomes. Stated differently, we focus on the leading indicators, not the lagging indicators. This is easier said than done, as outcomes are generally what are measured and what we are evaluated on. So, the idea of taking our eyes off the prize and onto something else takes courage.

Alan Mulally is a great example of this. Shortly after taking over as CEO, even though Ford was set to lose $12.7 billion, he asked the company to step up and invest more heavily in product innovation—the opposite of the cost-cutting approach so typical of those leading struggling organizations.

Mulally knew for Ford to right the ship, they needed to create products that were more attractive and appealing to their customers. In other words, Mulally knew the way back toward profitability was adding value to its customers. The more the company could do that, the more successful they would be. Product innovation was the system or process that would allow them to fulfill Ford's long-term purposes and goals.

4. Mind 3.0 People Have a Learning Goal Orientation

Think back to college or high school. What was your general goal for your classes? Was it to pass the class? Was it to get one of the best grades in the class? Or was it to learn and master the material?

Your answer reveals the goal orientation that you had back then. More than forty years of research has identified that individuals typically have on one of three goal orientations:

- **Performance avoid orientation:** The desire is to avoid the disproval of our competence and/or negative judgments about our competence. People with this goal orientation think, "I don't care about excelling; I just don't want to fail or look bad."
- **Performance approach orientation:** The desire is to prove our competence and gain favorable judgments about it. People with this goal orientation think, "I want to outperform my peers."
- **Learning orientation:** The desire is to develop skills and abilities, advance our learning, and master a task. People with this goal orientation think, "I don't care how I perform relative to others; I want to master the material."

The performance-avoid goal orientation is Mind 1.0 by nature. With this goal orientation, our focus is on doing the bare minimum required. It is safe, and there is no need to get out of our comfort zones.

The performance-approach goal orientation is Mind 2.0 by nature. Here, our focus is generally on doing as little as possible yet stand out. In a classroom setting, we do not care about learning the material; we just want to get a top grade. Thus, we generally only engage in surface-level learning strategies.

The learning goal orientation is Mind 3.0 by nature. Our focus is on developing ourselves. One of the key distinctions between those with a Mind 3.0 learning orientation and those with Mind 1.0 or Mind 2.0 performance orientations is our relationship with failure. Being in learning mode, we expect to fail and even welcome failure as a signal for progress. We have the cognitive and emotional sophistication to recognize that we learn and grow the most through failure.

Being in performance mode, we hate failure. To the Mind 1.0 performance-avoid leader, failure is a signal that we are incompetent. To the Mind 2.0 performance-approach leader, failure means that we are not the best and, therefore, of little value relative to others. In both of these stances toward failure, we commonly interpret failure as though *we* are a failure, and as such, we seek to avoid failing. In the process, we limit our long-term growth and development.

* * *

As I write this, I cannot help but think back on my educational experiences. During high school, undergraduate studies, and the first half of my doctoral program, I had a performance-approach goal orientation. I was focused on getting the best grades possible. Yet, I was also the epitome of doing as little as possible to get those grades. I was constantly looking for places where I could take shortcuts instead of investing in myself by mastering the material. To a certain degree, this served me well, as I received good grades throughout high school and my undergraduate studies. But this did not serve me well in my doctoral program.

When it came time to take my comprehensive exams mid-way through my program, I failed them. It was crushing at the time and, honestly, one of the low points of my life. But looking back on it now, it was a fantastic wake-up call. In my effort to regroup, I took on a *learning goal orientation*, and over the next year, I became focused on mastering the material. When I took my comprehensive exams the following year, I passed with flying colors.

Now, as a researcher who investigates the role of goal orientation in leadership effectiveness, I have learned the research on goal orientation has repeatedly found that, compared to those with either of the performance goal orientations, those with a learning goal orientation:

- Set higher goals and engage in greater effort to achieve them.
- Engage in deep-level (as opposed to surface-level) learning strategies.

- Seek out and are more receptive to feedback.
- Are more successful at adapting to change.
- Perform at higher levels.
- Are more likely to emerge as a leader and behave more effectively in a leadership position.

5. Mind 3.0 People Are Purpose-Focused

This is the birth child of the prior three characteristics. When we can see both the short term and the long term, when we can work the angles and keep sight of the outcomes while emphasizing the drivers of the outcomes, and when we can focus on mastery and deep-level development, it seems almost natural that we would be purpose-focused.

This is something we saw in the comparison between Steve Ballmer and Satya Nadella. During the first 90 percent of Steve Ballmer's tenure as Microsoft CEO, he had not worked toward crafting a purpose or a mission statement. This is not surprising, as a mission statement feels relatively unimportant for someone in Mind 1.0 or Mind 2.0, where the focus is on short-term performance-related outcomes.

On the other hand, the development of a clear mission statement was one of Satya Nadella's priorities after becoming CEO. He invested a year listening to Microsoft employees come up with the mission statement: "To empower every person and every organization on the planet to achieve more."

As a whole, I believe we can categorize Mind 1.0 as being comfort-focused, Mind 2.0 as being outcome-focused, and Mind 3.0 as being purpose-focused.

Think again about Microsoft's mission statement. Where is the focus? Empowering others. There is nothing in that mission statement about their own success.

6. Mind 3.0 People Are Intellectually Humble

When we are in Mind 1.0, we are afraid of being wrong because that might affect our sense of belonging to our group. When we are in Mind

2.0, we develop independent beliefs that we strongly believe are correct. Either way, in Mind 1.0 or Mind 2.0, we are generally focused on being seen as right. This makes it difficult for us to see the limits of our internal belief system and believe that we can be wrong.

When we function in Mind 3.0, on the other hand, we have enough cognitive and emotional sophistication neither to hold too tightly to our beliefs nor be seen as right. Holding a loose grip on our beliefs, we are willing to see, or at least investigate, the limits of our internal belief system. We believe we will always have incomplete information, and the more information we can get from varied perspectives, the better we will be at making decisions. Stated succinctly, we will be intellectually humble, which means we have a nonthreatening awareness of our intellectual fallibility.

Shane Snow, a thought leader on intellectual humility, identifies four components of intellectual humility. They are:

- **Having respect for others' viewpoints:** We do not disparage people whom we disagree with, and we seek to understand what has led them to believe in the way they do.
- **Not being intellectually overconfident:** We have a willingness to explore how we might be wrong, and we are willing to admit when we do not know something.
- **Separating our ego from our intellect:** We do not take it personally when we are shown we were wrong or were not aware of something, and we do not invoke experience, title, or other markers of authority to prove we are right.
- **Willingness to revise our own viewpoints:** We are gracious about conceding points to others, and we are willing to change our minds, even our firm beliefs, when given the evidence that we should.

What I have learned is that, in Mind 1.0 or Mind 2.0, we take a strong stance with our viewpoints. Our strong stance may feel right and serve us. After all, it helps us feel protected, secure, and confident. But it is not very cognitively and emotionally sophisticated. Ultimately, it is limiting.

When we are in Mind 3.0, though, we do not feel the need to take a strong stance on our viewpoints. We have learned that the looser the grip we have on our views, the more we can value new ideas and the views of others. And even if we do not agree with those ideas, we are generally better off simply because we exposed ourselves to these new ideas and viewpoints.

One area where our lack of intellectual humility shows is related to receiving feedback. When in Mind 1.0 or Mind 2.0, we are generally reluctant to seek out developmental feedback. Again, this is a self-protection mechanism. In Mind 3.0, however, we are much more willing and likely to seek out developmental feedback. At this level of development, we possess the cognitive and emotional sophisticated to recognize the long-term reward for doing so is worth any short-term discomfort that may occur.

A related area where our level of intellectual humility shows is when we make meaning of constructive criticism. In Mind 1.0, we typically see constructive criticism as an attack, so we get defensive. This is also true for when we are in Mind 2.0. Depending upon *who* delivers the constructive criticism and *how* they deliver it, we may also interpret constructive criticism as an attack against which we have to defend ourselves. In Mind 3.0, on the other hand, we possess the cognitive and emotional sophistication to recognize that even if the constructive criticism is not delivered effectively, there is probably something to learn from it.

It comes down to what we value. Do we value protecting ourselves, or do we value learning and developing?

7. Mind 3.0 People Are Psychologically Flexible

Have you ever seen someone get defensive to receiving constructive criticism? Get angry at a child for being childish? Bottle their feelings instead of being vulnerable? Pass the blame for a mistake they made? Get overly defensive about their children? Complain about a change? Resist an invitation to get out of their comfort zone?

Of course, we have never done these things ourselves (wink, wink), but we have surely seen others do these things. Why would anyone do these things? Well, in the heat of the moment, we are inclined to run with our emotional reactions rather than slow down and thoughtfully respond in a way that is more aligned with our personal values of being open, patient, responsible, agile, growth-oriented, and kind.

When we are psychologically inflexible, we hold rigidly to and behave in alignment with our emotions and reactions in the moment. But when we are psychologically flexible, we are no longer driven by our emotions and reactions. Instead, we possess the ability to connect in the moment, recognize the needs in the situation, and override our emotions or instinctual reactions to do what is best in the situation.

We all fall somewhere along the continuum between being psychologically inflexible and psychologically flexible. What research has found is that those who are psychologically more flexible have lower anxiety, depression, worry, and rates of substance abuse. They also have a greater ability to learn, a better quality of life, they perform better at work, and can better identify and describe their emotions.

To help you reflect on your psychological flexibility, consider these aspects of psychological flexibility and the related questions.

Psychologically Inflexible	Psychologically Flexible	Ask Yourself . . .
Experiential avoidance: You distance yourself from unwanted feelings and experiences.	Acceptance: You are willing to connect with unwanted feelings and experiences and learn from them.	How willing am I to contact unwanted experiences and learn from them?

Lack of contact with the present: You struggle to pay attention to your experiences in the given moment.	**Present Moment Awareness:** You possess mindful, attentive awareness in present moments.	To what degree am I able to stay present in the day-to-day situations I encounter?
Self as content: You see difficult thoughts and feelings as a reflection of yourself, leading to feelings of shame for having those difficult thoughts and feelings.	**Self as context:** You are able to maintain a healthy psychological distance from difficult thoughts. Difficult thoughts may occur, but they do not define who you are.	Is it easy for me to get wrapped up in difficult thoughts and feelings, or can I maintain a healthy psychological distance from them?
Fusion: You easily get trapped in unwanted internal experiences and inaction.	**Defusion:** You are able to step through unwanted internal experiences without getting stuck in them.	To what degree do I get stuck in unwanted internal experiences?
Lack of Contact with Values: You lose track of your priorities and values in the stress of the day. Your immediate needs override your values.	**Contact with Values:** You stay connected to your values and are continually driven by them. Your values override your immediate needs.	How easy is it for me to lose contact with my values?
Inaction: You easily get derailed by setbacks or difficult experiences.	**Committed Action:** You possess a resilient ability to move forward amidst setbacks.	How easy is it for me to get derailed?

Altogether, when we are psychologically inflexible, which is Mind 1.0 or Mind 2.0 programming, we are buffeted by our uncontrollable and feared internal experiences. But when we are in Mind 3.0 and are psychologically flexible, we do not hold tightly to any specific self-protective or self-advancing needs or fears. This allows us to be fully in touch with the present moment and the thoughts and feelings it contains without needless defensiveness. Instead, we can adapt to the needs of the situation and change our behavior in the pursuit of our goals and values. We can psychologically flex to the demands of the situation, allowing us to navigate the situations we encounter more successfully.

* * *

There is a great example of both intellectual humility and psychological flexibility in Adam Grant's book, *Think Again*. Grant is a well-renowned organizational psychologist. After giving a speech at a conference, the Nobel Prize-winning behavioral economist Daniel Kahneman came up to Grant, telling him how surprised he was at Grant's findings, as they contradicted Kahneman's research.

While most people in Kahneman's shoes might get defensive, Kahneman did the opposite. Grant said that Kahneman's eyes lit up and a huge grin appeared on his face, and Kahneman willingly admitted, "I was wrong."

Being surprised by Kahneman's response, Grant asked him why he seemed so joyful about being wrong. Kahneman responded by saying that he genuinely enjoyed discovering he was wrong because it meant he was now *less wrong than before*.

I do not think that Kahneman's way of thinking and acting is normal. In fact, it is rare. The only way he could so willingly admit that he was wrong, let go of his prior beliefs, and change his perspective is by being a Mind 3.0 leader and possessing both intellectual humility and psychological flexibility.

* * *

As you have been learning about the three mind levels, you will have noticed that the Mind 1.0 and Mind 2.0 internal operating systems are prone to react with defensiveness and resistance. Mind 3.0 internal operating systems, however, do not have that self-protective need.

You might be wise to identify the circumstances where you get defensive or resistant, as that might be a place in need of greater vertical development.

8. Mind 3.0 People Are Infinite-Minded

If we could boil down the characteristics and bright sides of Mind 3.0 into one statement, it would be this: People with Mind 3.0 internal operating systems are infinite-minded.

From the previous chapter, you may recall that when we are finite-minded, we see business and leadership as finite games with a beginning, middle, and end. Our goal is to win the game by beating out known opponents. It is a Mind 2.0 perspective.

On the other hand, when we are infinite-minded, we see business and leadership as an infinite game where the goal is not to win but to continue playing. The focus is not to be the best, but to exist in the best way possible into an unknown future. This is a Mind 3.0 perspective.

* * *

Allow me to give you examples from an individual level, corporate level, and national level to demonstrate how our perspective on the type of game we are playing influences how we process and operate.

HOW FINITE AND INFINITE MINDSETS AFFECT US AT AN INDIVIDUAL LEVEL

Think about how students approach their classes. When, as students, we possess a Mind 2.0 performance-approach goal orientation, we are playing a finite game. We see the class as having fixed rules, a beginning, and an end. With this finite perspective, our focus is on winning the game by getting the best grade in the class.

But when we possess a Mind 3.0 learning goal orientation, we are playing an infinite game. While the class may have fixed rules, we seek to use the class as an opportunity to better position ourselves for the future. The best way to do that is by learning and mastering the material in the class.

HOW FINITE AND INFINITE MINDSETS AFFECT US AT A CORPORATE LEVEL

Remember the difference between Microsoft's education summit under Ballmer's leadership and Apple's education summit? Microsoft's summit focused primarily on beating Apple. Apple's summit focused primarily on delivering value to the customer. Since Nadella has taken over, Microsoft is no longer focused on competing; they are focused on collaborating with their competitors in a way that allows them to best meet the needs of their customers. Hence, Nadella seems to be more infinite-minded.

HOW FINITE AND INFINITE MINDSETS AFFECT US AT A NATIONAL LEVEL

Consider the national warfare strategies of Germany and Japan during World War II versus that of the USA. During this war, wanting to win every battle, German and Japanese military forces generally kept their best fighter pilots on the front lines until they were killed. Justifiably, they were playing the finite Mind 2.0 game. But this limited their ability to be successful in the long run.

The United States, on the other hand, employed a strategy that pushed against the short-term strategy and pressure of seeking to win every battle. They were willing to sacrifice short-term success for long-term success. Rather than keep their best fighter pilots on the front lines, they systematically pulled them away from the front lines to train new pilots.

This strategy only makes sense from a Mind 3.0 infinite perspective, where the emphasis is not on beating out the competition, but on putting yourself in a better position to continue playing the game.

* * *

Can you see how, when we operate with a Mind 3.0 internal operating system, we possess the characteristics of being emotionally centered and balanced? We are also interdependent thinkers, emotionally intelligent, present, systems thinkers, learning goal-oriented, purpose-focused, intellectually humble, and psychologically flexible. Possessing these characteristics gives us a greater ability to see life as an infinite game, allowing us to navigate life more wisely and effectively, earning the apt description of a wise sage.

When I attempt to step back and soak in the combination of these characteristics, I see a blend of deep grounding, energetic agility, continual growth, and profound impact.

I also see that my internal operating system is not yet what it can be. Yet, at the same time, I appreciate seeing and understanding these characteristics. Doing so gives me increased clarity on the upgrades that I need to make and what a better version of myself would look like. This makes me excited for that future self.

MIND 3.0 LEADERS

After going through the hallmarks and characteristics of Mind 3.0, it probably would not surprise you that only 8 percent of executives and 1 percent of all adults operate at Mind 3.0. Together, these figures suggest that the odds of finding leaders and managers that primarily operate in Mind 3.0 is around one in twenty. But when you find them, those men and women seem to make magic happen, like Satya Nadella did at Microsoft and Alan Mulally at Ford.

The same can be said of Ed Catmull, the former president of Pixar and Walt Disney Animation Studios. Being in Mind 3.0, Catmull saw leadership as a responsibility of service. In his book, *Creativity, Inc.*, Catmull states:

> *The way I see it, my job as a manager is to create a fertile environment, keep it healthy, and watch for the things that undermine it. I believe, to my core, that everybody has the potential to be creative—whatever form that creativity takes—and that to encourage such development is a noble thing.*

For Catmull, leadership was not a vehicle to help him stand out, advance, and get ahead. Instead, it is a responsibility to contribute, add value, and lift others. Catmull did not hold on to power for fear of losing it; he was willing to give it away. Of this, Catmull also wrote:

> *I've made a policy of trying to hire people who are smarter than I am. The obvious payoffs of exceptional people are that they innovate, excel, and generally make your company—and, by extension, you— look good. But there is another, less obvious, payoff that only occurred to me in retrospect… By ignoring my fear [that these hires could one day replace me], I learned that fear was groundless. Over the years, I have met people who took what seemed the safer path and were the lesser for it.*

Catmull is suggesting that when we follow our self-serving Mind 1.0 desires of safety, comfort, and belonging or our Mind 2.0 desires of standing out, advancing, and getting ahead, we are the lesser for it. I believe this is something only Mind 3.0 leaders can see and internalize.

Mind 3.0 leaders stand apart from Mind 1.0 or Mind 2.0 leaders in at least three ways.

Mind 3.0 Leaders Are People Others Want to Follow

In Mind 1.0 and Mind 2.0, we are programmed to be self-focused. We commonly rely on organizational authority, rewards, or punishments to influence those we are leading to do what we want done.

But if we elevate to being Mind 3.0 leaders, we are programmed to be other-focused. We value our people as much, if not more, than ourselves. Our focus is on supporting and lifting those that we lead. We do not need to rely upon organizational authority or external incentives to influence.

By possessing the hallmarks and bright sides of Mind 3.0, we influence through our personal power, being people worthy of being followed. In fact, any organizational power we do have, we are willing to give to others as a way to empower them.

Mind 3.0 Leaders Are Dynamic

When presenting the three mind levels to organizational leaders, I inevitably get a Mind 1.0 or Mind 2.0 leader who asks, "To help balance out the perspectives, wouldn't you want Mind 1.0 and Mind 2.0 leaders on a leadership team?"

My response is always, "When you have a Mind 3.0 leader, you do not need any other type of leader because they can bring the parts of them that are best needed in every situation."

If the situation requires limiting risks, we can do that as a Mind 3.0 leader. If the situation requires pushing ahead, we can do that too. What allows us, as Mind 3.0 leaders, to be psychologically flexible comes from our ability to be both systems and interdependent thinkers.

In Mind 3.0, we can do two things that we would have struggled with in our days as Mind 1.0 and Mind 2.0 leaders. We can see and think below the surface and investigate the root causes of the problem. In addition, we can embrace conflict, paradoxes, and polarities. In doing so, we have the dynamic ability to do what the situation requires for us to add value—not what feels more comfortable or what will make us stand out. Our dynamism allows us to create sustainable solutions over longer-term time horizons.

Mind 3.0 Leaders Are Capable of Effectively Leading Change

As Mind 1.0 or Mind 2.0 leaders, we are simply not programmed to lead change. Operating in Mind 1.0, we are far too oriented toward protection and comfort to even seek or desire change. Instead, we resist change.

As Mind 2.0 leaders, we may be more open to change as long as it helps us be more successful. But because in Mind 2.0 we are short-term-oriented and have a hard time seeing systems and root causes, our efforts to bring about change are generally shallow and only incremental rather than deep and transformational.

It is only when we operate from a Mind 3.0 internal operating system that we can recognize something we could not appreciate in Mind 1.0 and Mind 2.0: Change is best brought from the top down. In Mind 3.0, being intellectually humble and psychologically flexible, we know that this means we need to change ourselves first before asking those we are leading to change.

Additionally, because we are more emotionally intelligent systems thinkers, we are more effective at communicating the purpose for change and altering established strategies, policies, and procedures that hinder the change we are seeking.

MIND 3.0 SUMMARY

Mind 3.0: Also known as contribution mode

Stats: 1 percent of adults operate primarily in Mind 3.0, and 8 percent of executives find themselves at this level.

Mind 3.0 Needs
- Contributing
- Adding value
- Lifting others

Mind 3.0 Fears
- Not being of value
- Taking from
- Limiting others

The Bright Side of Mind 3.0

- Mind 3.0 people are emotionally intelligent.
- Mind 3.0 people have a good relationship with time.
- Mind 3.0 people are systems thinkers.
- Mind 3.0 people have a learning goal orientation.
- Mind 3.0 people are purpose-focused.
- Mind 3.0 people are intellectually humble.
- Mind 3.0 people are psychologically flexible.
- Mind 3.0 people are infinite-minded.

Mind 3.0 Leaders

- Are people others want to follow
- Are dynamic
- Are capable of effectively leading transformation

* * *

Mind 3.0 is a categorization of an internal operating system that is both cognitively and emotionally sophisticated, to the point where it allows an individual's programming to transcend his or her inward desires to either stand in or stand out and, instead, be focused on having an outward impact through contributing, adding value, and lifting others.

Given that only 1 percent of adults and 8 percent of executives have been found to operate at Mind 3.0, it suggests that it is not easy to vertically elevate to this internal operating system. It requires loosening our grip on, if not altogether letting go of, any needs to be safe, comfortable, and belong (Mind 1.0) or to stand out, advance, and get ahead (Mind 2.0).

While elevating to Mind 3.0 is not easy and will not happen overnight, I believe the climb is worth it because we are able to become the highest version of ourselves. We will operate from a balanced and centered place that allows us to add the greatest value to the world we can add. And we will develop the bright spots of Mind 3.0 that will allow us to operate as a wise sage.

* * *

We have covered a lot of material in these three chapters, and to help you sit with this material and fully grasp the differences between the different mind levels, it is worth summarizing the three levels of development. That is what we turn to next, as I use a metaphor of a colony of penguins in frigid Antarctica.

CHAPTER EIGHT

THE THREE MIND LEVELS: A SUMMARY

Vertical Development Law #8

Leaders will operate at a lower altitude when their body budget is depleted, when they feel over-extended, stressed, tired, and/ or hungry. Leaders will operate at a higher altitude when their body budget is full.

The emperor penguins of Antarctica are incredible birds. They are the biggest of the eighteen penguin species and among the largest of all birds. Emperor penguins live in large colonies of as many as 10,000 birds.

In the dead of winter, female penguins lay a single egg that she oh-so-carefully passes off to her mate. She then walks up to seventy-five miles to get to the ocean to feed and store up food to regurgitate for the baby penguin. With food stored up, she makes the long hike back to the male. In all, this takes over two months.

Meanwhile, the male emperor penguin does one of the most remarkable things. Huddled together with thousands of other male penguins in what is called a *waddle*, he stands for the entire two months or more, keeping his focus singularly on keeping the egg warm. The temperatures are as low as -58°F and winds blow up to 125 miles per hour, so a single wrong move will instantly freeze and crack the egg. During that time, the male does not eat, and he loses half of his body weight.

* * *

Emperor penguins provide a useful context for explaining how people at Mind 1.0, Mind 2.0, and Mind 3.0 would operate if they were penguins—though not literally, of course.

MIND 1.0

Being programmed for safety, comfort, and belonging, Mind 1.0 penguins are primarily concerned with being at the center of their huddle. On the outskirts of the huddle, they are exposed to predators and cold, and may feel ostracized. But at the center, they feel safe, comfortable, and like they belong. As such, Mind 1.0 penguins are programmed to jostle for position or nudge others out of their way to get to the center of the huddle.

Mind 1.0 people operate much in the same way. They want to be integrated into their groups, and if their safety, comfort, or belonging is threatened, they will jostle for a better position regardless of the potential negative consequences for those around them.

MIND 2.0

If Mind 1.0 penguins are those that want to be in the middle of the huddle, Mind 2.0 penguins are those that stand apart from their waddle. They do not feel a need to be safe, comfortable, and fit in. Instead, they are internally programmed to stand out, advance, and get ahead.

Thus, Mind 2.0 penguins are inclined to go to an elevated position, a place where they can be seen and recognized by the group while also directing or leading them. And with their need to get ahead, if there are other Mind 2.0 penguins around, they are likely to compete against them to be in the most optimal position to be seen by and influence the waddle.

In the human world, it is also easy to see this Mind 2.0 phenomenon. While there are fewer Mind 2.0 people than Mind 1.0 people, because of their desire to stand out, the Mind 2.0 folks are often the most visible. They compete for higher status, bigger houses, nicer cars, more likes on social media, more votes, more subscribers, more fame, and more recognition within their sphere of influence. For them, the higher their position, the better.

MIND 3.0

If Mind 1.0 penguins are those in the huddle and Mind 2.0 penguins are those working to stand apart from and above the huddle, what do Mind 3.0 penguins look like? Allow me some creativity here, as Mind 3.0 behavior does not exist in a penguin colony.

Mind 3.0 penguins would not primarily be focused on themselves, whether standing in at the center of the huddle or standing out above the colony. Instead, Mind 3.0 penguins would be primarily focused on contributing to and improving life for the entire colony or pockets within it.

A Mind 3.0 penguin would recognize their colony is a long way from their food source. Their female peers are making harrowing long-distance journeys multiple times a year, during which their male peers effectively starve themselves to keep their eggs safe. With this recognition, a Mind 3.0 penguin would ask themselves, "How could I bring a food source to the colony?"

Solving this problem would become their purpose, and they would be driven to fulfill it. Being purpose-driven, they would sacrifice their safety, comfort, or belonging, and they would not engage in this work to stand out, advance, or get ahead. All they would really care about is: "Did I contribute, add value, and lift my colony?"

* * *

This imagery led me to asking myself what type of penguin I would be. As I look back on my adult life, I can clearly see that from when I was eighteen until I was thirty-three, I was a Mind 1.0 penguin. During that time, I was primarily focused on my safety, comfort, and belonging within my waddle.

I operated largely with a mentality of "How can I get through today in the easiest, most comfortable, and most enjoyable way possible?"

Even though I had big dreams, my operating system was wired for me to play small.

It was not until I began doing the research for my book, *Success Mindsets*, that I realized that while my self-protectiveness felt good and right, it was holding me back. So, I began working on improving my mindsets as a way of developing vertically.

Because of these efforts, I saw that I could level up to Mind 2.0. Elevating to Mind 2.0 led to me starting a consulting company, writing a book, and working to get my message out into the world. I worked hard to be a penguin that would advance my career, be recognized for my expertise, and win. My implicit perception was I would be valued by others for the work I was doing.

When I was thirty-six, I started learning about vertical development and the three different mind levels. I was convinced I was operating in Mind 3.0. After all, my consulting work and my book, *Success Mindsets*, were conscious efforts to contribute to my world, add value, and lift those around me.

However, the more I learned about Mind 3.0, the more I realized that I fell short of many of the Mind 3.0 characteristics. I realized that I was not being truthful with myself. I was not a Mind 3.0 leader. I was still in Mind 2.0. While I did feel I was working at contributing to others, I was doing it to be seen and recognized by others. If I was being honest with myself, being recognized was more important than actually contributing to and lifting others.

Although I did not like admitting that I was operating with a Mind 2.0 internal operating system, I appreciated the clarity. Not only did I feel I had a better sense of where I was, I also had a better sense of where I needed to go in my development. I needed to work on letting go of the fears and insecurities that had been causing me to hold on to the need to be recognized and focus more on simply being a contributor to others.

Since this realization of my lingering Mind 2.0 internal operating system, I have been working on upgrading to Mind 3.0. Although I have made some progress, I still feel I have some work to do. (More about my vertical development journey later.)

ASSESSING YOUR VERTICAL ALTITUDE

Think about this: Though I had been researching vertical development for a while, I was still able to fool myself to believe I was more elevated than I really was.

Hopefully, with this book, you will do a better job of self-assessment than I did. Between the description of the three mind levels and the penguin analogy, you should be able to get a good sense of your current vertical altitude and areas where you have opportunities to elevate.

I have one more tool to help you assess your vertical altitude. It is a tool I have found extremely helpful, and it is one you can use at any time or in any situation.

"Am I Above the Line or Below It?"

You may have heard the saying, "You have to name it to tame it." Everything we have covered related to the three mind levels is meant to help you name your vertical altitude so you can elevate. When we label levels of adult development, we can better know what levels we are at and be clear regarding the next steps in our development.

Below is a tool that can help you gauge your vertical altitude. It is a simple tool—a dotted line—but I have found it incredibly helpful with quickly assessing my current vertical altitude in order to make adjustments.

Mind 3.0
Contribution Mode
I want to contribute, add value, and lift others
INTERDEPENDENT THINKER

Mind 2.0
Self-Focused Reward Mode
I want to stand out, advance, and get ahead
INDEPENDENT THINKER

Mind 1.0
Self-Preservation Mode
I want to ensure safety, comfort, and belonging
DEPENDENT THINKER

Ask yourself, "When I am below that horizontal dotted line, where is my focus?"

It is on yourself—either your protection or your advancement.

Now, ask yourself, "When I am above that horizontal dotted line, where is my focus?"

In this case, your focus is outward. Your focus is on contributing to, lifting, or adding value to other people.

Knowing of these distinctions, you can check your vertical altitude by asking, "Am I above the line, or am I below it?"

Operating below the line is normal, even natural. That is the space from which 99 percent of all adults and 92 percent of all executives primarily operate.

The Conscious Leadership Group is a consultancy that focuses on vertical development. While they do not explicitly focus on the three mind levels, they do use this horizontal line tool. They suggest that being above or below the line is an either/or proposition. At any moment, you are either above the line or below it. They suggest, "If you are above the line, you are leading consciously, and if you are below it, you are not." It is that simple.

The Conscious Leadership Group also suggests:

Knowing when you are below the line is more important than being below the line. Leaders are in real trouble when they are below the line and think they are above it. This leadership blindness is rampant in the corporate world... [Yet, if leaders can] develop self-awareness and locate themselves accurately below the line, they create the possibility for shifting, a master skill of conscious leaders.

Their YouTube video on this topic is worth watching. It is called "Locating Yourself—A Key to Conscious Leadership."

CENTER OF GRAVITY

Everything related to the three mind levels we have covered has led to the implicit invitation for you to ask and answer a question that few people ever ask—and even fewer answer accurately: "What is my vertical altitude?" This is an incredibly powerful question, but it is not the only question we can ask ourselves related to these three mind levels.

If you are anything like me, one of the biggest challenges about answering this question is that you probably recognize all three mind levels in yourself. Thus, let me suggest a second question to ask that might help you feel more settled about evaluating your vertical altitude. Ask yourself: "Where is my center of gravity?"

While you might sometimes operate with lower or higher cognitive and emotional sophistication, you likely return to the mind level where you spend the greatest proportion of your time. That is your center of gravity. To gauge your center of gravity, it is helpful to ask: "What percentage of my time am I spending in each of the mind levels?"

This is not only a different way to assess your general altitude; it also leads to a productive and practical question related to your vertical development journey: "How can I spend a larger percentage of my time and life in Mind 3.0?"

My vertical development assessment is less of an assessment of your vertical altitude and more of an assessment of your center of gravity. It was designed to help you identify where you spend most of your time, and the place you are inclined to fall back to when you are feeling stress or pressure. As you sit with your vertical development assessment results indicating your center of gravity, I invite you to think about the times and situations where you tend to operate at a different altitude than what your assessment revealed. That can be equally revealing and insightful.

* * *

In the next chapter, I will share examples of what upgrading your internal operating system looks and feels like. These examples include stories from leaders I have worked with, leaders I have studied, and my journey of vertical development.

CHAPTER NINE

THE VERTICAL DEVELOPMENT JOURNEY

Vertical Development Law #9

Leaders do not primarily function at the highest altitude they have traversed. Instead, they operate somewhere between base camp and their highest climb. The level that leaders generally operate at is called their center of gravity.

Now that we are clear about the three levels of vertical development, let's explore what our vertical development journey entails.

CLIMBING A MOUNTAIN

To give you a sense of what our vertical development journey looks and feels like and the nuances involved, I will use a metaphor of climbing a mountain, where our altitude on the mountain is symbolic of our vertical altitude. Here are the foundational principles that are important to understand so you know what to expect on your vertical development journey:

- The journey up the mountain can be challenging, but it does not need to be. The difficulty of our journey is based on the speed of our climb and the route we choose. We can attempt to scale cliff faces, or we can take well-worn trails that have only a modest incline.

- Our journey starts at base camp. This is a Mind 1.0 altitude. According to vertical development research, this is where most adults find themselves. This is because it is safe and comfortable, and we are surrounded by many others, which helps meet our need to belong. When we are in Mind 1.0, the prospect of venturing up the mountain feels scary, dangerous, unnecessary, and lonely. At base camp, we fail to recognize that those who leave rarely come back. Thus, we also fail to appreciate the reason why most never return is that once you experience living at a higher elevation, you more readily see the limitations of living at a lower elevation.

- When we are in Mind 1.0 and are considering venturing up the mountain, not having a map can hold us back. Without a map, it is easy to let fear and uncertainty about the journey kick in. We might think, *What if I get lost? My effort will be a waste if I go the wrong route. What if I take a dangerous route instead of a safe one?* Often, the fear of not knowing where to go and the uncertainty about what we might experience can hold us back from venturing out and elevating up.

- Although venturing into the unknown without a map can be fearful, there are guides for our vertical development journey. They come in the form of mentors and books. We can always tap into those for direction. Also, we do not have to start the journey alone. There may be a chance to start with or follow others as they embark on their journeys.

- Along our journey, we will encounter obstacles, such as a cliff face. Cliff faces have their pros and cons. If you can climb up the cliff face, you will rapidly increase your altitude, but it takes significant effort, and it is dangerous. These obstacles leave us with the choice to turn around, find an alternative route, or confront the obstacle head-on.

     Whether we succeed at scaling the obstacle depends upon our current abilities and the tools we possess. As we scale smaller obstacles and succeed, we will grow in competence and confidence. But attempting to scale an obstacle and falling can be demoralizing. The less skill we have to begin with and the greater the fall, the more demoralizing it will be.

People who leave base camp but then come back are usually those who had a bad experience trying to overcome an obstacle. These returners either believe that vertical development is too hazardous or simply impossible. They resign themselves to mediocrity and give up trying.

- Once we start climbing, we take a tent. Wherever we pitch our tent is our home base. This is our center of gravity, the place where our mindsets and behaviors naturally default.

  We pitch our tents for a variety of reasons, which include taking shelter, taking a rest, storing up food and energy, and enjoying our newfound territory and scenery.

  With our tent pitched, we can always venture away from the tent. We can take short-term hikes up the mountain, down the mountain, or at our same altitude. But we will always come back to our home base. When we take hikes, we experience temporary changes in our state of mind. It is always easier to take hikes (i.e., experience a temporary change of mind) than to change our home base (i.e., change our internal operating system).

- One of the benefits of taking hikes up the mountain is that it allows us to see new things, experience new perspectives, and acclimate to the higher altitude, all of which can motivate us to continue climbing.

- Packing up our tent and changing our home base involves a complete paradigm shift and changes to our internal operating system. This can be a challenge. Not only is this a lot of work, but the prospect of leaving a place with which we have become familiar and acclimated can feel uncertain, even scary.

  This is especially true for those in Mind 2.0. In fact, those in Mind 2.0 generally love their current altitude, largely because they recognize they are higher than people at base camp; they are well acclimated to their current location, and they have experienced a lot of success at their current location. The prospect of leaving exposes a fear that they may not find the same success elsewhere. Thus, they are prone to feel they have risen enough, that rising further is unnecessary.

- The higher up the mountain we go, the fewer people we will encounter. But we will gain a better vantage point, offering new and better perspectives. This comes in the form of being a more complex, interdependent, and infinite-minded thinker.

- Wherever we are on the mountain, the primary force that slows us down or prevents our progress is our fears, especially the fears of failure, uncertainty, and being alone.

    The more we allow ourselves to awaken to and overcome our fears, the more willing we will be to awaken to and overcome our fears. In fact, if you have not gathered already, our vertical development journey involves an unceasing pattern of stepping into uncertainty, getting acclimated and pitching our tent, and then stepping into uncertainty again.

    The more we go through this pattern, the more confident we become in our ability to elevate. Thus, the higher we climb, the less daunting the climb becomes.

- The hardest parts of the vertical development journey are awakening to the limitations of our current level and the fears holding us back, and then mustering up the courage to let go of our fears and step into uncertainty.

- Finally, the higher we go in our vertical altitude, the greater our ability to positively influence others and make it easier for them to venture higher up the mountain. In short, the higher our home base, the greater our influence.

Let's now explore the major transition points on this vertical development journey.

GOING FROM MIND 1.0 TO MIND 2.0

Vertical development can occur at any age during adulthood.

While I was writing this book, I had a conversation with my wife's aunt, Karen, who is in her sixties. Karen is an incredibly bright woman who holds a doctorate in educational leadership. She spent the first half of her career as a nurse and the second half working in special education with stints as a principal and school district coordinator.

As we discussed my book, she confessed that she has experienced a significant change in her vertical altitude in the two years since retiring. I invited her to tell me more. Being vulnerable, Karen shared that she has realized two things she never appreciated before.

First, almost everything she did throughout her adult life was driven by an inner need to gain the approval of others. She acknowledged that whenever she did anything, whether it was teaching a class or baking cookies, it had to be perfect. She experienced a lot of anxiety and would go to great lengths to make sure she came across as polished so she could feel like she was of value to others.

Second, she realized she did not have a good relationship with herself. Deep down, she did not feel like she was of value, safe, and worthy of belonging. As a result, she sought out the approval of others so she would feel like she was of value, safe, and worthy of belonging.

Here she was, in her sixties, only now coming to the realization that she had a Mind 1.0 internal operating system. She is awakening to the fact that throughout her life, the decisions she made, the anxiety she felt, and the behaviors she engaged in were the result of self-protective programming. At the time, this programming not only helped her address her insecurities, but it also led her to do some really good work and receive accolades.

But now, she is beginning to see how this same programming that used to feel right was, in fact, holding her back from being the person she desires to be. She is now working on improving her relationship with herself so she can feel of value without the approval of others.

She can see that if she improves her relationship with herself, she will be less anxious and perfectionistic. And by being less focused on gaining the approval of others, she will become more focused on adding value to others, which will help her better contribute to her children, grandchildren, and church community.

As an observer of her vertical development, I am inspired by Karen's growth. She has been casting off the chains of insecurity, lowering her protective walls, and stepping into a brighter unknown.

HOW DOES VERTICAL DEVELOPMENT FEEL?

It is inspiring to witness the vertical development of others. But the development process is naturally uncomfortable and can be scary. To level up in our vertical development, we must:

- Let go of our need to be safe, comfortable, and belong, or our needs to stand out, advance, and get ahead.
- Investigate and push against our beliefs and assumptions about the world.
- Be willing to discover things about ourselves that we may not like.
- Embrace new ways of thinking and processing that are cognitively and emotionally unknown and uncertain.
- Change.

Doing these things is not something that comes naturally. What *is* natural is for change to be uncomfortable—even scary. I have heard people describe the process of mentally letting go of old beliefs and assumptions, embracing new ones, and changing our internal operating system as being gut-wrenching. But my experience is that it is never as painful as we anticipate.

* * *

A couple of years ago, I had two different therapies scheduled for one day. The first was a physical therapy appointment for a pulled calf muscle that was not healing as fast as I had hoped. This kept me from running.

The second was a meeting with a marriage therapist. At that time, my wife and I were working to close some distance that had grown between us.

Going into the day, I was looking forward to my physical therapy appointment. I anticipated this therapy would be painful—entailing exercise, stretching, and a massage of my damaged muscles—yet I almost looked forward to the pain because I knew it would lead to healing.

I did not feel the same about the marriage therapy appointment. I knew it would entail emotional stretching and the massaging of some sore spots in our relationship. I anticipated that it would be uncomfortable, and I did not look forward to it. I was happy to take the physical pain head-on, but I was reluctant to approach the possibility of emotional pain.

Sure enough, during my physical therapy session, they put me through the wringer, especially during the final third of the hour-long session. During that time, I received one of the most painful massages I have ever had. Apparently, my calf muscle was incredibly tight, and to loosen it, my physical therapist did some deep tissue massaging as well as a technique called cupping to promote blood circulation and relieve muscle tension.

I had to bite the towel I was lying on in order not to scream in pain. It was pure torture. After what seemed an eternity, my massage ended, and I was drenched in sweat from the amount of physical pain I had been put through.

While I hated going through it in the moment, I still viewed it as good pain, an investment in healing and my well-being. I would be better because of it.

Sure enough, a couple of weeks later, I was back to running.

As I limped out to my car that day, I remember feeling mixed emotions. Part of me felt accomplished for what I had just endured. But another part of me was dreading the marriage therapy that still lay ahead.

That evening, as my wife and I met with our therapist, she pressed into the pain points of our marriage, similar to what my physical therapist had done to my injured calf that morning.

As we delved into those painful areas, I became uncomfortably aware of some of the things I had done and was doing to cause pain in our relationship. Trying to slow myself down so as to not get defensive, the choice before me was clear.

I could go on defense and justify my perspective and behaviors as being valid, even though they caused pain in our relationship. Or, I could accept that my perspectives and behaviors, valid as they may be, were suboptimal and self-serving, and acknowledge that I carried significant responsibility for the distance in our marriage.

It must have been a good day, because I chose the latter. I allowed myself to see and acknowledge that my self-protectiveness was serving myself in some ways, but it was also causing me to be less attuned to my wife and behave in a manner that was causing us to drift apart.

Acknowledging how my actions negatively impacted my wife and our relationship was a hard pill to swallow. Honestly, it was deflating, humbling, and a hit to my ego. Just as with physical therapy, the process was painful, but as we left the therapist's office, I knew this pain was also a good pain, the type of pain that signified that healing was occurring.

Lying in bed that night, I reflected on the two therapy sessions. I had known that I could withstand the physical pain of physical therapy. Physical pain was something I was familiar with. I have always tried to push my physical boundaries in athletics, and I knew I got better and stronger when I did so. Which is why I was looking forward to the meeting with my physical therapist.

I was not as confident about my ability to embrace emotional pain. I was not nearly as accustomed to working through hard emotions, which made me apprehensive about meeting with the marriage therapist. Because I lacked the experience of pushing my emotional boundaries, I was not confident that I would get better and stronger when I did so.

If had a choice, I lay wondering, *which type of pain would I choose to go through again?*

The answer that came to mind surprised me. *I would choose the pain of marriage therapy.*

The emotional pain from the marriage therapy was, in fact, not as painful as the physical therapy. This has been a valuable lesson for me to learn, and I believe I am now much more willing to face and step into my emotional fears and pains, making me more willing to elevate in my vertical development journey. And as much as I love running, it is so much more meaningful to have a better relationship with my wife.

* * *

On your vertical development journey, you will experience similar feelings as I did. You will stretch your emotional and cognitive muscles. It will not be easy, and it will likely cause ego-related pain, which is uncomfortable—even scary. But while it will not be easy or comfortable, it is doable. And it is worth it.

I am convinced that you will not find this growth as difficult or as scary as it may feel going into it. And on the plus side, the results will be both meaningful and life changing.

GOING FROM MIND 2.0 TO MIND 3.0

Meet Sal, a client of mine. Sal is the founder and CEO of a mid-sized and growing organization. He is charismatic, passionate, and demanding. Everybody likes Sal.

Sal has been a successful leader. His organization had recently been recognized as being one of the fastest growing companies in the region. They had grown 200 percent over each of the previous two years.

I went into our first coaching call expecting it to be like what I generally experience with executives, where I find a lot of posturing, fear avoidance, and justification. So, I was pleasantly surprised when Sal was open and willing to be transparent and vulnerable.

Early in the call, I asked Sal, "Why did you start your business?"

Here is where he first surprised me. He said, "To prove others wrong." Later in the conversation, he added, "I try not to let anyone see this, but deep down, I am a very insecure person."

This was not the first time I heard these words from a CEO, and I am sure it will not be the last.

If someone were to tell you they started their business to prove others wrong and that they were an insecure person, what mind level do you think they predominantly operate from?

Probably Mind 2.0.

Sal is not too different from many business leaders who see business success as a way to help them feel secure, worthy, and valued.

While his center of gravity is in Mind 2.0, this is not to say that he does not operate at Mind 3.0 at times, because he does. He can even revert to Mind 1.0 at other times.

But since we have been working together, Sal's challenge has been to continue to develop his relationship with himself so that he can be more secure. Until such a time, his internal operating system will chase after standing out, advancing, and getting ahead.

While Sal's Mind 2.0 internal operating system has led to a certain level of business success and likely makes his leadership style feel right or good to him, it has not come without its unintended negative consequences.

With a strong drive to advance and grow, Sal tends to be impatient with his employees. And as the organization has been growing, he has been having a hard time delegating. I have also observed that he tends to think in the short term and has difficulty seeing the bigger picture. So, while the organization has hit some major milestones, they are not yet in a position to secure long-term success.

As Sal's leadership coach, I find it both inspiring and encouraging that he is wrestling with these issues. Sal is becoming increasingly more open to investigating his beliefs and assumptions, pushing against them, and developing a more outward-oriented and purpose-focused internal operating system.

Specifically, he is beginning to see that his need for success causes him to put the business before people—including his family and himself. He is also starting to realize that as the organization grows, he has to grow along with it. He cannot continue to be personally involved in every proposal and every project. He has to loosen the reins and trust others.

Considering the mountain metaphor, I would describe Sal's home base as long having been established at the Mind 2.0 level on the mountain. He is connected to this place and identifies with it.

Letting go of a location that feels like home is not easy, but Sal is beginning to see that his current home is not as great as he once thought it was. He has been taking short hikes up to Mind 3.0 levels. He is in the beginning stages of shifting his home base to a higher altitude.

In doing so, Sal is having a mixture of feelings. There is some grief involved in the letting go of what is familiar. There is some anxiety around the uncertainty of setting up a new home base and forging new ways of making sense of the world. But with that comes some excitement about the prospect of being a better person and a better leader.

I believe the mixture of these feelings is a great signal that Sal is headed in the right direction on his vertical development journey. What an honor it is to guide him on this journey.

* * *

I would imagine that you are ready to learn how you can develop vertically, how to upgrade your internal operating system so you can become more of the person and leader that you long to be.

The rest of this book is dedicated to helping you do that. And in learning how *you* can develop vertically, you will also learn how you can help *others* do the same.

Giving you that clarity and guidance is the focus of the remaining chapters of this book.

PART TWO

———

How to Develop Vertically

CHAPTER TEN

THE KEY TO VERTICAL DEVELOPMENT

Vertical Development Law #10
Leaders' foundational meaning-makers are their mindsets. These are their mental lenses that filter the information that comes into their brain, interpret that information in unique ways, and activate the elements about themselves to best navigate the situation based upon the information filtered in and how it is interpreted.

I spent more than ten years studying leadership and leadership development at a deep level before I came across these vertical development ideas that I present in this book. So I would imagine that vertical development is a new concept to you too.

Having learned about vertical development and the three different mind levels, you may have asked yourself—like I have—why we place so much emphasis on horizontal development and why vertical development is not talked about more.

The short answer is that most leadership-development thinking has been built on short-sighted and faulty assumptions that have long gone unquestioned and untested.

ASSUMPTIONS IN SCIENCE

All scientific tests involve assumptions. The reason we make assumptions in science is that it is difficult to control 100 percent of factors that may affect an outcome. So if these assumptions go untested—which happens more often than we care to admit—we can draw incorrect conclusions. This, in turn, leads to poor decision-making and sometimes catastrophic disasters.

The Challenger Space Shuttle incident is a prime example of scientific assumptions going untested, in this case leading to the shuttle breaking apart barely more than a minute after takeoff.

The incident was caused by a couple of O-rings that failed. O-rings are used to create a seal where two parts are connected, keeping liquid or gas from escaping or entering. Typically, they are made of rubber as it can expand or contract, thus forming a proper seal.

In the case of the Challenger, NASA scientists had conducted many tests to verify that the O-rings worked properly. For each test, they made assumptions about various factors, including that the temperature does not affect the effectiveness of the O-ring. They also assumed that on launch day, the temperature would not be significantly different than when the O-rings were tested.

But January 28, 1986, launch day, was unseasonably cold. This prevented the O-rings from expanding adequately, which led to the explosion.

While there were some at NASA who were aware that temperature *might* pose a problem to the functionality of the O-rings, the collective knowledge at NASA was based on faulty assumptions left untested.

Another example is when Barry Marshall and Robin Warren tested the assumption that ulcers are caused by stress and poor eating habits. They found that the presence of ulcers has little to do with one's lifestyle and almost everything to do with the presence of a type of bacteria called *Helicobacter pylori*. This discovery led to Marshall and Warren being awarded the 2005 Nobel Prize in Physiology or Medicine.

As a result of these men testing the assumption around the cause of ulcers, we are no longer given antacids or undergoing surgery for the treatment of ulcers. Instead, we are given antibiotics to kill the bacteria.

From these two examples, we can now see that assumptions are a part of the scientific process, and it is not uncommon for people or fields of study to hold onto unproven and untested assumptions for a long time, though they may be neither valid nor accurate.

Let us now consider some foundational assumptions in leadership development that have led to an overemphasis on horizontal development and an underemphasis on vertical development.

ASSUMPTIONS IN LEADERSHIP DEVELOPMENT

Leading up to World War II, psychologists made a couple of monumental advancements that have influenced psychological thinking and research ever since.

They developed theories of intelligence that suggested people vary in their intelligence and that people with more intelligence can be more effective than people with less intelligence. And then they developed methodologies to assess people's intelligence. At the time, this led to the improvement of appointing people—military personnel in particular—to positions where they were likely to be successful.

Ever since, psychologists have been enamored with identifying other personal traits or characteristics that influence how people behave and how effective they are.

The Trait Approach

As more and more psychologists began studying leadership, the focus expanded beyond intelligence to include other personal traits, like personality, as well as various leadership styles. Over time, the dominant question asked and studied by leadership researchers has been, "What are the traits and styles of the most effective leaders?"

The purpose of answering this question has been to help organizations have greater clarity regarding what to look for when selecting leaders and what to focus on when developing leaders.

This led to the identification of a host of leadership styles and associated traits and characteristics found to be important for effective leadership, including authentic leadership, charismatic leadership, transformational leadership, and servant leadership.

While this approach has led to a large body of leadership knowledge that we have benefited from to some degree, it carries an assumption that few have questioned. And as with the O-rings on the Challenger, this assumption can have devastating consequences.

The assumption is called the trait assumption. **The trait assumption suggests that leaders manifest their traits, styles, and characteristics in the same form and fashion across all the situations they encounter.** In other words, if a leader has a trait such as charisma, the assumption is that they will be charismatic across all situations they encounter.

Does this assumption feel accurate to you? Unfortunately, it carries several significant limitations:

1. It views the variability of leaders' behaviors across situations as being either a measurement error or an internal contradiction.
2. It views situations as being mutually exclusive and irrelevant to leaders' manifestation of their traits.
3. It overlooks and fails to address all the psychological processes and dynamics that underlie leaders' behaviors.
4. It fails to consider that leaders can operate in consistent patterns across similar situations, but might operate in very different ways in different situations.

Overall, the trait approach ignores an important reality: **the person and the situation are inextricably interwoven**. While leaders' traits influence how they operate, leaders do not employ their traits to the same degree across all situations.

Many of our current leadership philosophies are based upon the trait approach. As a result, our leadership development efforts have primarily been horizontal development efforts: downloading certain traits, characteristics, knowledge, and skills like one would download an app onto an iPad. We have believed that leaders would then employ these traits consistently across all situations.

By predominantly relying upon the trait approach, the leadership development community has largely failed to appreciate the role context plays in how leaders employ their knowledge, skills, and traits.

The Situation–Trait Approach

More and more, leadership researchers have started to include the context—the situation—into the equation, taking on what is called the situation–trait approach. This shift has been promoted as a renaissance in the leadership domain.

The situation–trait approach carries several assumptions:

- It assumes that a leader's context or situation has a significant influence on the expression of their leadership.
- It assumes that leaders possess a wide variety of traits, which include knowledge, skills, personality attributes, and self-regulatory strategies, and that leaders do not utilize all these traits across every situation.
- It assumes that, depending upon the factors present in the situation, leaders will activate some traits and deactivate others to best navigate their situation.
- It assumes that leaders develop unique patterns of processing and behavior such that when they encounter situations similar in nature, they will activate similar traits and operate similarly across those situations. But if they encounter situations different in nature, it is likely that they will activate different traits and operate differently across those situations.

To bring these assumptions to life, consider introverts. Do introverts demonstrate their introversion to the same degree across all situations they encounter? No. If they are at an event with strangers, they may act introvertedly. But if they go to an event with family and friends, they will generally activate more of their extraversion tendencies.

Central to the situation–trait approach is the idea that people possess within themselves encoding processes. While the psychological field explicitly uses the label "encoding processes," this is the same thing that I labeled and described as our sense-making system earlier in this book.

Our encoding processes operate within our brain, generally automatically and below the level of our consciousness. As you will come to see, these encoding processes are vital to how we see, think, and operate. In fact, they have three primary jobs.

The first job of our encoding processes is to scan the situation we are in for any cues that may be relevant for informing how we should operate in that situation. For example, if I were to step onstage to speak to a room full of women, I would likely be quick to take in that information as being valuable to me in navigating that situation most effectively. When cues are identified as being salient, we pass them further into our mind for further processing, leading to the next job of our encoding processes.

The second job of our encoding processes is to interpret and give meaning to the cues that were identified for further processing. If I pick up on the fact that my audience is a room full of women, I could potentially interpret that as being scary or safe depending on my experience working with women.

The third job of our encoding processes is then to activate the different traits about ourselves that will allow us to best navigate the situation based upon the cues taken in and how they are interpreted. For example, if I interpret my speaking situation as being scary, I might become protective and clam up. But if I interpret my speaking situation as being safe, I might loosen up and focus less on myself and more on adding value for the audience.

This leads to a final assumption of this situation–trait approach: every leader will differ in how they read, interpret, and make meaning of their situations. In other words, leaders possess different encoding processes, and these encoding processes can differ in their cognitive and emotional sophistication.

The encoding processes function at the intersection of our situation and the activation of our traits. As such, they are the most foundational reason for why we do what we do. How we read, interpret, and make meaning of our situations is what activates select traits from our portfolio of traits. This, in turn, leads to our response to the situation.

Our encoding processes are where our internal operating system resides. They drive how we make meaning of our world around us. And they are programmed to make meaning of our world in a way that is most supportive of the needs we possess at our vertical altitude.

For Mind 1.0 people, encoding processes are programmed to help us ensure our safety, comfort, and belonging. For Mind 2.0 people, they are programmed to help us stand out, advance, and get ahead. And for Mind 3.0 people, they are programmed to help us contribute, add value, and lift others.

* * *

Our encoding processes explain why my son likes to watch recordings of his sporting events. They allow him to make meaning of the situation as an opportunity to learn. My daughter, on the other hand, does not like watching recordings of her sporting events. When she reluctantly does so, you can see her nervous system take over and go into protection mode. This is because she makes meaning of the situation as an attack on her competence and abilities.

For both of my children, their interpretation of the same situation is automatic, yet it dramatically shapes their cognitive and physical responses in opposite ways.

Comparing the Trait Approach and Situation—Trait Approach

The approach we as leadership developers adhere to significantly influences how we go about helping leaders develop. When we adhere to the trait approach, believing that traits drive behaviors and that leaders manifest their traits to the same degree across all situations, we generally focus on one or both of the following for development:

- **We will focus on helping leaders develop specific traits** that we know are helpful for leadership effectiveness. These traits might include charisma, integrity, emotional intelligence, empathy, confidence, positivity, or adaptability.

- **We will focus more directly on improving leaders' behaviors,** helping leaders do the things that people with effective leadership traits do. This approach is generally structured as how-to trainings, such as how to deliver effective feedback, how to create psychological safety, how to engage or motivate employees, how to provide recognition, and how to delegate effectively.

Whether the focus is on traits or behaviors, such development can be classified as horizontal development. And as we have stated earlier, this type of development can be incrementally helpful, though it will always be limited as it does not address leaders' underlying operating systems.

When we adhere to the situation–trait approach, though, believing that how leaders encode their situations dictates the traits they use and the behaviors they engage in, we are no longer as interested in simply improving leaders' traits and behaviors. Instead, we are interested in improving and upgrading leaders' encoding processes and how they read and interpret their situations.

Implied in this approach is an empowering belief: leaders may already have the traits and abilities to function effectively, their effectiveness just needs to be unlocked through an upgrade in their internal operating system.

When the focus is on improving leaders' encoding processes, we are doing vertical development. We are elevating leaders' ability to make meaning of their world in more cognitively and emotionally sophisticated ways.

THE KEY TO VERTICAL DEVELOPMENT

You may have been wondering how you can help yourself or others develop vertically and what you need to focus on to do so.

The answer is to focus on the encoding processes, the parts of ourselves that make meaning of our world with a certain level of cognitive and emotional sophistication.

But what exactly are our encoding processes? They are our mindsets. Many people consider our mindsets to simply be our attitudes toward something. For example, people refer to an "entrepreneurship mindset," implying a certain attitude toward being entrepreneurial. But our mindsets are so much more than that.

In the next chapter, I will go into greater depth on what mindsets are. For now, suffice it to say, **our mindsets are the mental lenses that dictate how we see and view the world**. Our mindsets selectively organize and encode information, thereby orienting us toward a unique way of understanding an experience and guiding us toward corresponding actions and responses.

When we focus on developing leaders' mindsets, we are engaging in vertical development. We are elevating the sophistication of their meaning-makers and upgrading their internal operating system so they can react to, encode, and process their world in more healthy and effective ways.

* * *

Earlier (in Chapter Eight), we talked about how leaders at different levels of development respond to constructive criticism. When someone operates in Mind 1.0, they make meaning of and encode constructive criticism as being an attack. This interpretation will lead them to become defensive and closed to constructive criticism. In doing so, we label them as having a *closed mindset*.

In developing leaders, if we want someone to respond more effectively to constructive criticism, we need to help them develop an *open mindset*, a Mind 3.0 characteristic. Operating with an open mindset, they will have the cognitive and emotional sophistication to make meaning of and encode constructive criticism as being potentially valuable information.

SUMMARY

Most leadership development efforts stem from leadership thought and research founded upon the trait approach. The trait approach carries with it the incorrect assumption that leaders manifest their traits in a similar fashion across the various situations they encounter.

Assuming the trait approach is accurate has led leadership developers to focus on the horizontal development efforts of improving traits and behaviors, something that is just incrementally helpful.

In contrast, the situation–trait approach to leadership development suggests that the traits and behaviors leaders employ are contingent upon how they encode their situations. When we see the flaws in the trait approach and assume the situation–trait approach is accurate, we will alter our focus away from horizontal development efforts of improving traits and behaviors and employ more vertical development efforts focused on improving the sophistication of leaders' encoding processes and their meaning-makers: their mindsets.

* * *

In the next chapter, we will take a deep dive into what mindsets are at a neurological level. In doing so, we will gain clarity on how to help ourselves and others develop vertically. This will involve a crash course in neuroscience, so buckle up for an interesting journey.

CHAPTER ELEVEN

THE NEUROSCIENCE BEHIND VERTICAL DEVELOPMENT

Vertical Development Law #11

When leaders operate at a higher vertical development altitude, they are okay looking bad in the process of learning and growing, they are okay being wrong in the process of finding truth and thinking optimally, and they are okay wading through problems to reach their purpose-fueled destination. They are also okay putting themselves on the back burner if it means that they can better lift others. These behaviors may not make sense to those who are less vertically developed.

What part of the body controls and dictates how we process information, make decisions, and operate? The mind. This is also where mindsets reside and where vertical development occurs.

Although this might seem obvious, how many leadership development programs have you been a part of that focus on the mind? In most cases, when I have asked leaders this question, they respond with either "none" or "very few."

Given that the mind controls a leader's effectiveness and is where vertical development occurs, the lack of focus on the mind in leadership development is problematic.

But we can rectify that.

The simple reason why in leadership development we do not focus on the mind much is that most leadership development efforts are based upon dated philosophies, dated research, and dated assumptions. In fact, I believe it is safe to say that most leadership development efforts used today are rooted in philosophies and research that were developed before 2005. That year is significant because this is roughly the year that neuroscience went mainstream.

Searching ProQuest, the most comprehensive academic database, I discovered the following trend:

- From 1960–1974, only eight articles contained the word *neuroscience*.
- From 1975–1989, that grew to 152 articles containing the word *neuroscience*.
- From 1990–2004, the number jumped to 9,040 articles.
- From 2005–2019, the number of articles rose exponentially. In that timeframe, 142,842 articles containing the word *neuroscience* were published.
- And in 2020 and 2021 alone, there were 41,000 articles published that contained the word *neuroscience*.

We have learned more about the mind since 2005 than we have known in all the years before that. And as most leadership development programs were developed before 2005, they could not have had a strong focus on the mind. As a result, the mind has largely been absent from leadership development—not because we have purposely overlooked it, but because we did not know enough about it to focus on it. That is, until recently.

It is time for us to bring the mind into the leadership development equation.

UNDERSTANDING THE MIND

A Quick Caveat

Many experts in the field of neurology have argued that the human mind is the most complex structure in the universe. So when we talk about the mind, we do so in grossly simplified terms. Doing so helps us to make sense of it, though our understanding will always be limited and not necessarily completely accurate.

In what follows, we will use models and analogies to help make the neuroscience behind vertical development palatable. Please remember that there is far greater complexity and nuance to discover.

Neurons and Neural Connections

The fundamental building blocks of the mind are neurons. A neuron is a brain cell that passes electrical impulses to other neurons by way of strings of neurons called neural connections. **Nearly everything the body does is a result of the brain sending electrical signals via neural connections.**

Our brains are divided into different regions. For the most part, neural connections stay within the region of the brain where they are housed. But there are also select neural connections that span and connect regions of the brain.

The Triune Brain

One of the most well-known models of the brain is the triune brain model. This model suggests that the brain has three regions—the reptilian, mammalian, and human brains. While each region performs countless jobs, we will focus on the role that each region plays in the meaning-making process.

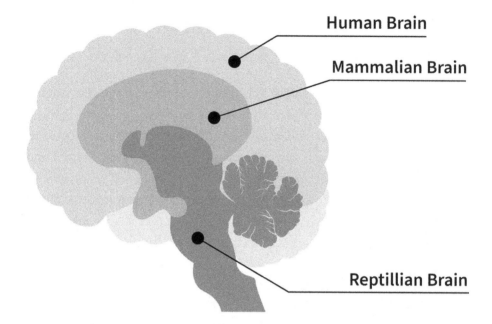

The reptilian brain is the most primitive part of our brain. It is at the top of the spinal column and is made up of the brain stem, the cerebellum, and the basal ganglia. This is the part of the brain where our body sends all information first.

One of the primary jobs of the reptilian brain is to be alert for any signals of danger. When such signals are received, it will immediately activate our stress-response system, slowing or shutting down most other processing in order to maximize our response to the danger, which generally manifests in us as a fight, flight, or freeze response. After the reptilian brain has filtered the information, it passes that information to the higher, more sophisticated levels of the brain.

The mammalian brain is the next layer up in the brain. It is made up of the hypothalamus, amygdala, and hippocampus. The mammalian brain is largely where our implicit memories lie. It is the place in the brain where we construct meaning of the signals that are sent to it. This tapping into memories to make meaning of our situations in real time occurs automatically and nonconsciously.

For example, imagine seeing a clown. How you interpret or make meaning of the character will be based upon your experiences with clowns. If you have seen the movie, *It,* for example, you might remember scenes from the movie and interpret a clown as being scary. But if you grew up going to rodeos and seeing rodeo clowns, you will access more positive memories related to clowns and will be more inclined to interpret them as being funny rather than scary.

The human brain is the cerebral neocortex. It is the outside region of the brain. One major function that it serves is to bring consciousness, awareness, and rational thought to our meaning-making process. But it may not always do so because the stimuli first pass through our reptilian and mammalian brains. If either of these brain regions senses danger, they will activate our body to respond before we get a chance to consciously process our situation.

Ideally, these three major regions of the brain will work together in the meaning-making process. The better they work together, the greater the possibility for greater accuracy in the meaning-making process.

Accuracy is critical in meaning-making. If our accuracy is off and, say, we interpret a safe situation to be dangerous or a dangerous situation to be safe, we will navigate our world less effectively than if we had been more accurate in our meaning-making. Our level of inaccuracy will lead us to perform in a manner that is not appropriate for that context.

For example, as mentioned, when we function in Mind 1.0, we respond to constructive criticism as though we are being physically attacked, causing us to respond in a manner that may feel justifiable but is ultimately unproductive.

Unfortunately, our ability to make meaning accurately is constrained by:

1. Our inability to take in all information—a limitation of our reptilian brain
2. Our limited life experience and memory reserve, which could have been potentially damaged through trauma and/or neglect—a limitation of our mammalian brain

3. Any inability that we may have in allowing our human brain to play a conscious and regulating role in the meaning-making process

Long-Range Neural Connections

For these brain regions to communicate effectively and work together, there are long-range neural connections that span the three regions. These long-range neural connections are central to our meaning-making—they are our mindsets.

To illustrate how the three brain regions work together, we will use the clown example again. When you see a clown, your body sends your reptilian brain information regarding what you are seeing. Your reptilian mind will process the information, filtering it along with related information to the mammalian brain.

When your mammalian brain gets the information from the reptilian brain, it will then automatically and nonconsciously make an interpretation of the signal based upon your past experiences, recalling whether a clown is scary or funny.

This interpretation will start the process of activating your body's response based upon your interpretation. But in the process of doing so, the human brain can step in, slowing down and even altering the body's instinctive response.

If you interpreted the clown as being scary, your body will immediately go into stress-response mode. Your heart will beat faster, and the hair on your arms may stand up. But if your human brain steps in and helps you realize that what you are seeing is only a picture and the clown is not actually present or real, your brain will recognize you are not in immediate danger. Thus, it will help you regulate your physical and emotional responses to seeing the picture of a clown.

Without the human brain's intervention, you may have overreacted to the situation.

* * *

The neurological processes described here are the same as what we described in Chapter Ten regarding our encoding processes:

Step 1: Filter in important information.

Step 2: Interpret that information.

Step 3: Activate a response to the situation based upon the information filtered in and how it was interpreted.

Our understanding of the encoding process comes from the field of psychology. But what we are now establishing is that neuroscientists are independently confirming the accuracy of the situation–trait approach at the neurological level.

When we combine the psychological perspective and the neurological perspective, it becomes clear that our mindsets are long-range neural connections that both facilitate communication between the three major regions of the brain and operate as our encoding processes, dictating how we make meaning of our world. As such, **both psychology and neuroscience have identified mindsets as being the most foundational aspect of why we process information and operate the way we do.**

Integration and Disintegration

By now, it should be clear that your brain and mine make meaning of our world in distinct ways. These ways of making meaning can be categorized along a continuum, from being less cognitively and emotionally sophisticated to more cognitively and emotionally sophisticated.

We are now able to understand why—on a neurological level—one leader will overreact to a team member's mistake while another leader will grow curious about the same mistake. The difference lies in *integration* and *disintegration*—terms that psychologists and neuroscientists use to explain how our three major brain regions work together.

When a brain is integrated, the long-range neural connections are of such quality that they allow for all three brain regions to work together effectively. No brain region overpowers another, allowing for accurate and sophisticated meaning-making and higher-quality response processes.

When a brain is disintegrated, it means that the long-range neural connections are inhibited such that the three major brain regions do not work together as effectively. In disintegration, the reptilian and mammalian brains tend to operate on overdrive, and the human brain is unable to step in to regulate the processing of information in those brain regions. This commonly results in less accurate and less sophisticated meaning-making and response processes. Psychologists call this having an overactive or overly reactive stress response. Effectively, our core regulatory network is inhibited.

We gain two valuable insights by understanding integration and disintegration:

- The quality of our mindsets and our ability to make meaning in the most effective and sophisticated way is contingent upon the integration of our long-range neural connections.
- At a neurological level, vertical development involves improving the quality of our long-range neural connections so they can do a better job of integrating our minds and improving our self-regulatory abilities.

Integration, Disintegration, and Leadership Effectiveness

Michael and Jim are both managers in the finance department of a large real estate developer. Michael's team is responsible for the western region, and Jim's team is responsible for the eastern region.

While Michael and Jim seem similar on the surface, they are not the same on a neurological level. Michael's mind is less integrated than Jim's. As a result, Michael vacillates between Mind 1.0 and Mind 2.0. He possesses more negative mindsets, and he is less vertically developed than Jim.

What this means is that Michael's overactive reptilian and mammalian brains cause him to be triggered easily. Situations that commonly trigger him are when his image and reputation can be called into question. Thus, as a nonconscious protection mechanism, Michael focuses on making sure that everyone on his team is performing at an acceptable level and that there are no problems.

One day, Michael receives a phone call from the CFO letting Michael know that a report submitted by one of his team members was incorrect, which led to under-budgeting a job. The CFO found a decimal point in the wrong spot on one of the figures in the estimate. While this seems like a small error, it cost the company thousands of dollars on the project.

During the call with the CFO, Michael's lower brains were operating on overdrive, interpreting the call as a signal that he was a failure as a manager. Michael was certain that he would either be fired, demoted, or forever stuck in the same position. He was convinced his reputation was shot.

Having been triggered, as soon as Michael hung up the phone, he quickly headed over to the team member responsible for the error and berated him for not double-checking his work. Michael left that conversation feeling justified. He even felt a little safer having firmly placed the blame for the error on someone other than himself.

Jim, on the other hand, is more integrated. As a result, he has more positive mindsets and is more vertically developed, generally operating in Mind 3.0. Jim is not unconcerned about his image, but when he is in a situation where his image or reputation might be called into question, while he might feel defensive at first, he possesses the ability to slow down and regulate those feelings.

In fact, Jim experienced a very similar situation just a few months prior to Michael's incident. Jim's team was responsible for putting together some projections for a meeting between the CEO, CFO, and a potential client. As these parties were going through the finances of a deal that was on the table, it became clear that the numbers were inaccurate. This ultimately led to them losing the deal and thousands of dollars in revenue.

The CFO called Jim to inform him of what occurred. Jim felt sick to his stomach, and his lower brains started to analyze what implications this might have on his future with the company. But after the call, Jim was able to connect to his human brain, allowing him to devise an intentional strategy for moving forward instead of just instinctually reacting.

Being in a more settled state, Jim went through the report, investigating where the errors occurred and what he missed before he had sent the file to the CFO. Once Jim found the errors, he approached the entire team involved in creating the report—not just the person most responsible for the errors.

During this meeting, Jim explained the situation. He shared the blame with all parties involved in creating the report. Jim asked questions to better understand what about their processes led to this error, and he gathered ideas for how they could improve moving forward.

Jim knows that he and his team are better because of this experience.

THE CONNECTION BETWEEN VERTICAL DEVELOPMENT, MINDSETS, AND INTEGRATION

Unfortunately, in real life, Michael's response is more common than Jim's response. It is this difference that leads to commonly reported abysmal leadership statistics, including that 75 percent of employees say their direct leader is the most stressful part of their job, and 60 percent of employees report that their leader damages their self-esteem.

But based upon what we have covered, we know that Jim's response is rooted in these realities:

- Jim is more cognitively and emotionally sophisticated than Michael.
- Jim possesses more positive mindsets than Michael.
- Jim's mind is more integrated than Michael's mind.

In all, the difference between Michael and Jim as leaders is that Jim is more vertically developed than Michael.

* * *

Once we understand that the foundational difference between good leadership and bad leadership lies in how vertically developed leaders are, it becomes frustrating that very few leadership development programs focus on vertical development.

In fact, in surveying 153 organizations about their leadership development programs, I found that only 12 percent focused on mindsets. Of the 88 percent of organizations that reported they did not focus on mindsets, only 29 percent reported they were effective at developing their leaders. Contrast that to the 12 percent of organizations that reported that they did focus on mindsets. Of them, 67 percent reported that they were effective at developing their leaders. In other words, **organizations that focus on mindsets seem to be more than twice as likely to be effective at developing their leaders.**

This is clear: if you want to work on your vertical development or help others with their vertical development, you need to focus on the integration of your mind and on improving your mindsets. Later, we will discuss how to do this. Before we get to that, it will be helpful to explore your current degree of integration as well as how you came to possess your current mindsets. Once you know how your brain has become wired the way it has, you can better understand how to improve its wiring.

CHAPTER TWELVE

HOW OUR MINDSETS FORM

Vertical Development Law #12

Elevating leaders' vertical altitude requires an investigation of how they make meaning of their world and why they make meaning in the ways that they do. This generally involves a rejection, release, or surrender of current worldviews and the acceptance, adoption, and reassertion of new worldviews. It is as much about dismantling as it is about forging.

In my experience as a consultant and coach, one client who stands out as having the keenest business mind is Sharon, the head of development for a large tech company.

Sharon is intense, nonstop, and always in control. During our Zoom calls, Sharon commonly paced around her office building, laptop or phone in hand, her image on my screen bouncing up and down.

On our first call, to help me understand what she desired from me as a consultant, Sharon spent the first twenty minutes passionately sharing her strategy for her division and its success. She informed me that to win in their industry and ensure business growth in the long run, the priority had to be on developing products faster than anyone else, and those products had to be of greater quality than anyone else's.

Next, Sharon told me her priorities in descending order. I do not remember all the items, but I do remember that speed and quality were at the top and cost was at the bottom. Sharon was adamant that cost was of low concern to her because she believed it was fine to spend more money if the return was greater speed and quality.

A lot of what Sharon told me that day was brilliant. It was inspiring to hear her articulate her vision and talk about what she was doing and where she was going. But keeping in mind her constant pacing, her firm beliefs, and her assertiveness, I wondered what it would be like to work for Sharon. I had the impression that she operated more like a battering ram than a leader.

When Sharon finally got around to telling me why she wanted to bring me in to work with her division, my first impression of her was confirmed. She had a team of young leaders, and while they were very capable, they were not keeping up with her. She was looking to me to help elevate her team. She wanted them to be faster, more willing to take initiative, and more agile. She felt a focus on mindsets would do the trick.

Between what Sharon was saying and the tone with which she said it, it felt like she simply wanted me to fix her team. But I also picked up on something she did not talk about—her role in her team's struggles. It was as though Sharon was saying, "I am not the one that needs help, it is my team that needs help."

Sharon finally slowed down enough for me to speak. I told her I would be happy to work with her team and that I thought I could help create the outcomes that she desired. But I gave her a caveat. I told her that the outcomes would only come about if she saw herself as part of the team and was involved in the development efforts as much as her team members, if not more. I also explained that team members generally do not buy into leadership development efforts if they perceive their leader is not also invested in their own development.

I got the impression that Sharon had not planned on being involved in the development efforts, but she saw the value of it, so she agreed to go on the development journey with her team.

Part of the work I ended up doing with Sharon and her leadership team involved surveying all the team members' subordinates about their supervisor. That way, they would receive feedback about the quality of their leadership, mindsets, and vertical development from those they were leading. The information gathered from those surveys would lead to several coaching calls, during which I would go over the feedback and do some personalized vertical development and mindset work.

In Sharon's case, it meant her team had to respond to a survey about her as a leader. They also had to share their perceptions of her mindsets and level of vertical development.

Unsurprising, the feedback on Sharon's leadership was not positive. Her team expressed concerns about her having expectations that were too high and being guilty of micromanaging them. A common observation was that if Sharon felt a project was going slower than she expected, she would interject herself into the process. Typically, she would start having frequent meetings with the team member about the progress of the project. Her team complained that having to spend more time in meetings with Sharon about the progress of the project slowed down the project even more.

Occasionally, Sharon would take a different approach. She would push the team member aside and assume responsibility and leadership of the project. This was especially demoralizing to her team.

This feedback led me to wonder about two things:

1. What mindsets were driving Sharon to interject herself in unhealthy ways?
2. Why did Sharon possess these mindsets in the first place?

To me, unreasonably high expectations and the tendency to micromanage staff were signals of disintegration, a Mind 2.0 internal operating system, and a need for vertical development.

Understanding the neuroscience behind mindsets, I recognize that we develop our mental wiring and associated mindsets to successfully navigate our world. Thus, while Sharon's mindsets might have helped her get where she was when I met her—that is, in a high-profile position doing important work with a great company—I knew some of her mindsets might be preventing her from getting where she wanted herself and her team to go.

To help Sharon develop vertically, I would need to better understand her disintegration by identifying her blocking or limiting mindsets. Finally, it would be helpful for me to understand why she had developed those mindsets in the first place.

Identifying blocking and limiting mindsets is a critical step in the vertical development process because it not only diagnoses the problem, but it also brings clarity on how to treat the issue most effectively. For me, understanding the why behind her mindsets would help me understand how to help her develop vertically via improving her mindsets and enabling greater integration.

We will come back to Sharon at the end of this chapter, and then again at the end of the next chapter. First, let us explore where mindsets come from.

WHERE DO OUR MINDSETS COME FROM?

One of the questions I most commonly get asked is how people come to possess their current mindsets.

To fully answer this question, we will take a three-part journey. First, we will take a step back and take a closer look at the brain so we can better understand the wiring of our mindsets. Next, I will share with you two mechanisms that shape the wiring and mindsets in our brain. We will cover both of these parts in the remainder of this chapter. The third part will be covered in the next chapter, where we will look at the role trauma plays in our mindsets, integration, and vertical development.

* * *

Earlier, we established that our mindsets are long-range neural connections. These neural connections vary in size, our largest neural connections being sixty times larger than our smallest neural connections.

The formation and strength of our neural connections is based primarily upon *nature*, not *nurture*. In fact, it is helpful to think about our mindset neural connections as being like muscles. The more we use them, the stronger they become. This is where the phrase, "Neurons that fire together, wire together" comes from. In other words, the formation and strength of our mindset neural connections have been formed through use over time.

Further, the larger a neural connection is, the stronger it is, and the more readily and rapidly it will fire. Thus, when a neural connection is strong and can fire readily and rapidly, we will rely upon that neural connection more dominantly as a part of our default and natural patterns of processing.

Over time and through our life experiences, the wiring in our mind develops into something similar to a road system. Most of the signals that pass through the brain go through our largest neural connections—the highways, if you will. But there are also boulevards and side streets that are not used as much.

How, then, did we come to form the wiring we currently have? To answer simply, we come to possess our mindsets through our life experiences and our current culture.

Our Life Experiences

When we focus on the role our life experiences play in shaping our mindsets, we are looking at a broad window of our past, however long that may be.

The most formative part of our mental development is during childhood, but we also have significant experiences as adults that can dramatically alter our mindsets and the associative wiring in our brain. This can be for the negative or for the positive.

Child psychiatrist and neuroscientist Bruce Perry, Ph.D., partnered with Oprah Winfrey to write *What Happened to You? Conversations on Trauma, Resilience, and Healing*. Perry and Winfrey report the first two months of our lives have a disproportionately important impact on our long-term health and development.

> *If in the first two months of life, a child experienced high adversity with minimal relational buffering but was then put into a healthier environment for the next twelve years, their outcomes were worse than the outcomes of children who had low adversity and healthy relational connection in the first two months but then spent the next twelve years with high adversity.*

They go on to say that even though research bears this finding out, it does not leave us powerless from creating greater health and development throughout our lives. Our brains are pliable. We can create new neural connections.

While the quality of our mental wiring and mindsets as adults have strongly been influenced by the earliest experiences in our lives, experiences throughout the rest of our lives can also influence our mental wiring and mindsets.

The reality is that we are social and surviving creatures. We are willing to adapt so we can navigate through our environments socially, emotionally, and physically unscathed. In doing so, we are inclined to develop wiring that allows us to best survive the settings in which we find ourselves. That is Mind 1.0 wiring at its finest.

Since we are raised in different contexts, we develop different wiring to survive our childhood environment. A child neglected by his parents may develop wiring that seeks approval and recognition. A child abused by her parents may develop wiring to be a people-pleaser. And a child raised with loving and supportive parents will develop less self-protective wiring.

But our wiring cannot only be attributed to our experiences during our formative childhood years. In my research on mindsets, I found that widowers—compared to those who are married, divorced, or have never been married—generally develop more compassionate wiring. At the same time, they are also more self-protective in that they are more sensitive to experiencing problems and situations that might expose their lack of competence or ability.

* * *

I recently had a coaching call with an executive approaching the tail-end of her career. She is someone who acknowledges she struggles to connect with her employees. In diving into why that was, she was quick to tell me a mantra her father used to repeat: "People generally take themselves too seriously and their work not seriously enough."

How she interpreted this is that when you are at work, work. Do not allow anything, particularly relationships and emotions, to get in the way of doing high-quality work.

She has been carrying around this mantra and mindset her whole life, and she has never really questioned or pushed against it. She has never stopped to consider if it was valid, if there are aspects about it that are helpful, or if there are aspects about it that have unintended negative consequences.

She finds herself now leading employees and having a very difficult time navigating the various emotional struggles they are experiencing.

My main invitation to her as the next step in her vertical development journey was to question this mantra, identify its pros and cons, and consider whether there is a different mantra that might better serve her as a leader.

I hope this gets you to think, "What mindsets, stories, and mantras are guiding my life, yet going unchecked and possibly limiting me?"

Another client recently told me that a mantra he heard in his house growing up was: "You can have love or money, but you can't have both." Does that feel very cognitively and emotionally sophisticated to you? Do you think that holding on to this mantra would set this person up for success or disappointment?

In all, our life experiences shape our mindsets. But we also need to consider our current culture.

Our Current Culture

In *Atomic Habits*, James Clear shares a great example of the power of context and culture on how people operate. Research on U.S. soldiers stationed in Vietnam during the Vietnam War found that 35 percent of service members had tried heroin, and as many as 20 percent were addicted to it.

Upon returning from Vietnam, only 5 percent of the previously addicted users became addicted again within the first year of being home, and only 12 percent relapsed within three years. Essentially, nine out of ten soldiers who used heroin in Vietnam eliminated their addiction seemingly overnight.

When we step into a new setting, be it a workplace, religion, sports team, or geographic region, we are on high alert to pick up on and adhere to the cultural and social codes of conduct within that group or region. We know if we operate in alignment with their social codes, we are more likely to fit in and be socially unscathed. If we choose not to do so, we put ourselves at risk of being treated as social outsiders.

In the case of the drug-using Vietnam soldiers, the social pressure to avoid drug use was not as strong or as prevalent in Vietnam as what they found upon returning home. Returning soldiers must have picked up on social cues that informed them that to reintegrate honorably, they would need to give up their drug usage.

When we step into a new culture, we will likely find the social code of conduct differs from our natural way of operating. At a neural-connection level, it requires that we intentionally activate less-dominant wiring to navigate the situation effectively and safely. Then, the more and more we operate within that culture, our less-dominant wiring is strengthened, making it a more dominant part of our processing. In all, the social pressures built into a culture serve to rewire our brain, causing us to take on different mindsets, at least for that cultural setting.

* * *

When I help organizations assess the quality of their leaders' and employees' mindsets, we often look at the quality of mindsets across tenure levels. What I commonly find is that if their employees have strong positive or negative mindsets—suggesting a strong corporate culture for that type of mindset—there will be a clear trend across tenure levels showing that as tenure goes up, employees' mindsets morph to match either the strong positive or strong negative mindsets.

I saw this when I worked for Gallup. Prior to working there, I saw Gallup as a thought leader in the human resources space and assumed they would have a culture of creativity and innovation. In my year of working there, though, what I observed was that the culture was neither creative nor innovative.

While Gallup may have once been more creative and innovative, what had happened over time was they had learned that if they made mistakes or had errors on their reports, they would lose credibility with their clients. As a result, the culture at Gallup came to focus more on avoiding problems than on delivering value. They had what is called a prevention-minded culture.

So, when I first started working at Gallup, what I experienced and what I observed with other new hires was that we wanted to push the boundaries, try new approaches, and innovate. But from the broader culture, the social cues of avoiding problems and getting things right stifled these desires. New hires may have come into Gallup more promotion-minded, but since the culture socially incentivized being prevention-minded, these new hires gradually took on more of a prevention mindset.

* * *

Not only can our mindsets shift over time to align with the culture of a group, it is possible for us to activate and rely upon certain mindsets in one culture and different mindsets in a different culture. Just think about how you operate at work versus at home.

If there is a context that we operate within (say, at work) that requires mindsets that differ from our dominant ones (our mindsets at home), it is possible to bounce back and forth between these mindsets depending upon the context. When this occurs, what is going on in our brains is that cues from one context activate certain mindsets, but cues from another context activate different mindsets.

I see this most commonly when there is an area of someone's life that is significantly more psychologically safe than another area. For example, if someone feels psychologically safe at home, they are more inclined to operate with more positive mindsets in that setting. But if they do not feel psychologically safe at work, as soon as they step into the work context, they will activate more self-protective and negative mindsets. It is a protective mechanism.

The Wiring to Survive May Not Be the Wiring Needed to Thrive

The development of our mindsets, whether as a byproduct of our past experiences or current culture, generally happens naturally and lies below the level of our consciousness. We take on mindsets that will help us socially, emotionally, and physically survive the situations we are operating in. If those situations require self-protection, we will take on self-protective mindsets. These mindsets will feel good as they will serve our self-protectiveness. In fact, they will feel so good and so right that when someone suggests an alternative mindset, we will likely resist that idea because—given our past experiences or current culture—it will feel wrong. It will be like telling someone who lives in a crime-ridden area not to lock their car doors.

Think about it. What type of response would you get if you told everyone at work they should start doing a better job of embracing problems as it is impossible to get from where you are now to where you want to go without encountering problems? I do this every week in my work with organizations, and from my experience, I can tell you the response is typically resistance and plenty of eye-rolling.

I usually follow that exercise with this question: "Will the mindsets that helped you survive your upbringing or current culture allow you to succeed outside of those contexts?" The answer is generally no.

From this perspective, it is easy to see that what worked in the past may not work in the future. The mindsets that helped us survive thus far are unlikely help us thrive.

I have personally learned the hard way that the mindsets I developed to survive my childhood did not help me much as an adult. In general, they negatively impacted my ability to be an effective employee, leader, spouse, and parent.

What makes this challenging is the leaders I generally work with are people who have demonstrated success in their past and are quite confident in the effectiveness of their current mindsets. They have every reason to be confident. But then I come along and suggest that some of the mental wiring they have developed to succeed thus far may limit their effectiveness moving forward. Only in a few instances did the leader I was coaching *not* resist. Instead, leaders almost always justify their perspective. That is okay. I expect mindsets and related beliefs will be difficult to inspect, question, and adjust, especially since they had served them so well in the past. But that same resistance is what is generally holding them back from operating at a higher level.

Take Sharon for example. To her, her high-ranking position and relative success is validation that she is exceptional, leaving her with little interest in considering whether or not she possesses some rough parts that might need some refining.

Initially, she resisted my efforts to get her to inspect and question her mindsets. I view such resistance as a justifiable defense mechanism, so I seek to create a safe space for clients to offer resistance and try my best to validate their perspective. In the process, they grow to trust me, their walls come down, and they open up more, often sharing stories about past trauma.

When I first started coaching executives, what they shared with me in this safe space surprised me. But after hearing similar stories time and again, I am no longer surprised by clients' vulnerability.

Generally, what lies at the root of leaders' negative mindsets is a story of past trauma. This came up so frequently that I have engaged in an in-depth study of trauma and how it affects our mindsets and vertical altitude. What I learned from this has not only been insightful, it has been life-changing. In the next chapter, we take a closer look at the impact trauma has on the wiring of our brain.

CHAPTER THIRTEEN

TRAUMA: ITS EFFECTS ON OUR MINDs AND OUR LEADERSHIP

Vertical Development Law #13

The less vertically developed leaders are, the more resistant they are to vertical development. The more vertically developed they are, the more leaders recognize the importance of vertical development.

Dr. Nadine Burke Harris is the author of *The Deepest Well*, one of the most revolutionary books on trauma. In this book, she writes about her time as a research assistant in a tadpole and toad lab at the University of California, Berkeley. They were exploring the role various hormones had in the growth and metamorphosis of tadpoles into toads.

Hypothesizing that the stress hormone corticosterone might influence gender development, Dr. Harris and her team injected tadpoles with this hormone. They were unable to find that it influenced gender development. Instead, they found it influenced other aspects of the tadpoles' metamorphosis.

Wanting to replicate this finding under natural conditions, the team created a situation that caused tadpoles to naturally produce high levels of corticosterone: they placed them in a container with many other tadpoles and not enough water.

The team hypothesized that the stress-activated release of high levels of corticosterone would speed up the tadpoles' metamorphosis. But this was not always the case. What they found was if the tadpoles were past a certain point in their development into toads, the stressful conditions did, in fact, lead to an acceleration in their metamorphosis. But if the tadpoles were early in their development, the stress inhibited their metamorphosis.

Specifically, Dr. Harris and her team found that if too much corticosterone was released early in the tadpoles' development, it caused hormonal dysregulation, throwing their biological processes out of whack. Specifically, the corticosterone knocked out the thyroid hormone, which had two catastrophic side effects: it inhibited the tadpoles' metabolism, preventing them from growing, and it affected the production of surfactant, which plays a key role in lung development and helping tadpoles absorb oxygen out of the air.

In other words, the tadpoles' stress response to overcrowding was adaptive if it happened at the right time during development. But if the stress exceeded what the tadpole could handle at an early developmental level, it had catastrophic consequences.

Dr. Harris draws a clear parallel between the effect of stress on tadpoles and the effect of trauma on humans: trauma is at the root of most, if not all, vertical development limitations. **This interplay between vertical development and trauma is so strong that we cannot address vertical development without addressing trauma.** Ignoring the impact of trauma on vertical development is like driving a car that is missing a tire; you might be able to go from one place to another, but the journey will be neither efficient nor pleasant.

WHAT IS TRAUMA?

Most people consider trauma to be a really bad event or experience that sticks with you and can have an enduring impact on you. But this perspective is incomplete because a "bad event" is subjective. During the height of the COVID-19 pandemic, it was not uncommon to hear people say the pandemic and related shutdowns were traumatizing, but not everyone found their experience to be traumatic.

An event or experience is only traumatic if it disrupts or alters the wiring in our brain and our related nervous system. Thus, **trauma is less about what we experience and more about how our bodies react to what we experience.**

To fully understand how our bodies respond to trauma, we need to take a look at our stress-response system, a vital system within our nervous system. Our body's stress-response system is designed to protect us from harm or danger, and it does this in several different ways.

Imagine you are standing at the edge of a cliff. Your nervous system will sense danger and activate the release of stress-response hormones like adrenaline and cortisol to prepare your body to respond to the danger. You will feel the effects of your stress-response system when you notice your hands become sweaty, the hair on your arms stand on end, and your heart rate speeds up, preparing your muscles for action.

Our stress-response systems can also influence our memory formation. For example, when my daughter was three, she had a lamp on her nightstand. One night, after I read her some books and turned my back to her, she reached into the lamp and grabbed the lightbulb. The pain resulted in an immediate howl. She was clutching her hand in pain from a burn across her palm and tiny fingers.

Even though this happened more than seven years ago, my daughter is still leery of getting close to lamps. In this instance, her stress-response system helped my daughter's mind bookmark this experience as an important memory, one that would help keep her safe in the future.

* * *

Experiencing stress and activating our stress-response system is not necessarily a bad thing. We have probably all experienced how stress can push us to operate at a higher level. We have also likely recognized that once minor stress or danger has passed, our body has the ability to regulate, stabilizing our body and mind to counteract the effects the stress hormones initially had.

But what is vital to realize is that our body's stress-response system has a load limit. Our stress response and regulation systems can only handle and manage a certain amount of stress effectively, and this load limit is different from person to person.

When we experience stress that falls below our stress-response system's capacity, it is generally resilience-building. It leads to a stronger and more flexible stress-response capability that increases our capacity for taking on stress in the future.

But when we experience stress that exceeds the capacity of our body's stress-response system, our body goes to extreme measures to protect us and limit pain. These measures involve dramatic alterations to the wiring in our mind, such as disintegration, described in Chapter Twelve.

Researchers have found that trauma-induced wiring alterations have predictable and long-lasting consequences. These effects do not have to be long-lasting, though, as efforts to heal from the trauma can, yet again, rewire the mind.

In connecting trauma to mindsets and vertical development, it is vital that we understand these consequences. Before we get into them, it will help to understand the three primary categories of trauma that lead to alterations in the wiring of our minds, and the consequences thereof.

The first category is prenatal stress. This usually occurs when a pregnant mother engages in or is a victim of stress-inducing behaviors such as drug or alcohol use, physical abuse, etc.

The second category is prolonged stress, commonly referred to as little-t trauma. This occurs when someone experiences prolonged stress that is uncontrollable and unpredictable. Possible examples might include divorce, surviving a natural disaster, or working in a toxic environment.

The third category is significant stress, commonly referred to as big-T Trauma. Significant stress involves experiences that are intensely stressful. Examples might include someone experiencing physical or sexual abuse, seeing someone murdered, or surviving a catastrophe.

Recognizing these three categories of stress-induced trauma helps us to see that trauma is not just the result of intense experiences, but also the pattern of experiences.

Unfortunately, statistics suggest that if you have not experienced one of these forms of trauma, you are the exception.

Assessing Trauma and Its Impact

One of the standard ways researchers have investigated the consequences of trauma throughout our lives is by connecting the number of adverse childhood experiences (ACEs) to various life outcomes, including premature death and various health conditions and mental disorders.

The ACE assessment asks whether individuals have experienced any of ten adverse experiences during childhood. These include being physically or verbally abused, sexually assaulted, or neglected; having experienced parental separation or divorce; having lived with an alcoholic, a drug user, or a depressed person; or having a household member in prison.

ACE scores are helpful for research, but they are limited in that they do not include more minor traumatic experiences, nor do they include traumatic experiences encountered as adults.

Among all adults, 61 percent reported that they have experienced at least one ACE, while 16 percent report experiencing four or more ACEs. ACE-related research has repeatedly found that the higher our ACE score, the more negative life experiences we have later in life.

As children, those with ACE scores of four or more are thirty-three times more likely to have learning and behavioral problems compared to those with a score of zero. And as adults, they are twice as likely to experience heart disease, twice as likely to develop autoimmune diseases, four-and-a-half times more likely to be depressed, ten times as likely to be intravenous drug users, and twelve times as likely to be suicidal.

Dr. Harris compares experiencing childhood trauma to exposing children to lead. Both affect the long-term development of our brain. Being exposed to high doses of stress and trauma is especially toxic. Such stress and trauma not only causes people to be less healthy, less resilient, and more prone to disease, but they also prevent people from experiencing trust, intimacy, motivation, and meaning.

Factoring in trauma that can occur during adulthood, researchers estimate that at least 70 percent of adults have experienced at least one traumatic event in their lives. Many experts point to this high rate of experienced trauma as being at the root of many of our bodily, mental, and social ills.

THE CONSEQUENCES OF TRAUMA ON OUR MENTAL WIRING

Our body is designed to keep us alive in the face of trauma. Thus, when we experience trauma, our body enters self-protection mode. Not only does this occur at the moment of trauma, but the self-protective effects linger at a foundational neurological level such that after we experience trauma, we are more conditioned to think and operate in a manner that is focused on surviving the present moment.

The degree to which trauma influences our mental wiring differs from person to person based on factors that include genetic vulnerability, the developmental state at which the traumatic events occurred, and the history of previous trauma. The buffering effect of healthy relationships, family, and community also influence our mental wiring's capacity. Regardless of these factors, though, we do not walk away from trauma without our mental wiring being affected.

In fact, trauma has four common and predictable consequences on how we see and make meaning of our world, others, and ourselves. I call these the four dominoes of trauma due to the impact one consequence has on the next.

Dissociation

The first domino is dissociation. When we experience a situation that exceeds our stress-response capacity, our body's natural reaction is to cut off, or dissociate, ourselves from the experience and any fear or pain we might be experiencing.

A common form of dissociation is numbing. Numbing, along with other dissociative responses, involves a disconnection between our mind and our body. This helps us survive in the moment, but it often leaves lasting neurological damage. While this disconnection can prevent terrifying sensations from being felt, dissociation does not simply cut off terrifying sensations. Instead, it tends to cut off or limit all sensations, even positive ones. As a result, our relationship with our inner reality becomes impaired.

As Brené Brown astutely points out: "We cannot selectively numb emotions; when we numb the painful emotions, we also numb the positive emotions."

Trauma researcher Bessel van der Kolk describes this powerfully in his best-selling book, *The Body Keeps the Score*: "Knowing how much energy the sheer act of survival requires keeps me from being surprised at the price [trauma survivors] often pay: the absence of a loving relationship with their own bodies, minds, and souls."

Disintegration

Cutting off the connection between our body and feelings tips the second domino: disintegration.

As alluded to before, the first major change that occurs in the brain as a result of trauma is the reptilian and mammalian brain areas go into overdrive while the human brain shuts down, all in an effort to limit and control the terrifying and lingering sensations of trauma. The area of the human brain that is deactivated is the medial prefrontal cortex, responsible for our executive functions such as planning, decision-making, and personality expression.

Also, there is abnormal activation of the insula, which is located in the mammalian region of the brain. The insula is a part of our limbic system and is responsible for integrating and interpreting input from the body. When the insula is more active than normal, it causes us to be on edge, unable to focus, or have a sense of imminent doom.

The combination of these two changes is disintegration. With our reptilian and mammalian brains being oversensitive and operating in overdrive, our human brain is unable to step in and regulate or integrate the input.

A common metaphor to describe the effects of disintegration is of a rider and an unruly horse, with the human brain being the rider and the reptilian and mammalian brains being the horse. As long as the path is easy, the rider can feel in control. But the horse is easily agitated, and if spooked, it will bolt, forcing the rider to hold on for dear life, with little ability to reign in the horse.

This second domino of disintegration knocks down the next two dominoes simultaneously. These dominoes are misencoding and shrinking our window of tolerance.

Misencoding

In Chapter Ten, we discussed how psychologists have identified our encoding processes as being the most foundational aspect for why we do what we do. After we experience trauma and dissociation and disintegration occurs, our ability to encode our world accurately becomes inhibited. This is what I call *misencoding*.

A common byproduct of trauma is that it causes us to encode our world as more threatening than it really is. In other words, those who experience trauma become more prone to seeing safe things as dangerous and experiencing something psychiatrist Daniel Goleman was the first to refer to as an *amygdala hijack*—when our amygdala obstructs our human brain from functioning as it should. What psychologists and therapists have learned is that traumatized people look at the world in a fundamentally different way than people who have experienced little to no trauma. Trauma survivors tend to superimpose their trauma on everything around them and have trouble accurately deciphering what is going on around them.

When traumatized people work toward and become more integrated, they realize what they most trusted—their self-protective minds—were, in fact, working against them.

Seeing safe things as dangerous can be incredibly limiting. Ideally, we want our stress-response system to be an accurate detector of safety and danger. We do not want to be caught unaware by a raging fire, but if we are unable to regulate every time we smell smoke, it will be intensely disruptive.

The Shrinking of Our Window of Tolerance

The final consequence of disintegration is the shrinking of our window of tolerance, a domino that falls side-by-side with misencoding.

The term *window of tolerance* is attributed to Daniel Siegel, M.D., to describe a zone or state of arousal where a person's brain is functioning well and is effectively processing stimuli. When we are within this zone or state, we are able to readily receive, process, and integrate information and respond to the demands of everyday life without feeling overwhelmed or withdrawn. Also, it is only in this state that we can be present and mindful. It is the optimal zone for us to operate within.

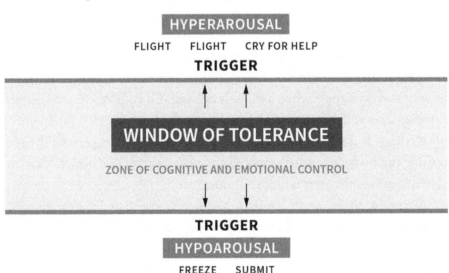

On the top edge of our window of tolerance is hyperarousal, a state characterized by hypervigilance, feelings of anxiety, and racing thoughts. On the bottom edge of our window of tolerance is hypoarousal, a freeze-response state characterized by feelings of emotional numbness, emptiness, or paralysis. When we are in either of these states, we cannot accurately process stimuli, be present, or be mindful, and we are inhibited from responding to life in an effective manner.

When we experience stress, our mental state gets pushed toward either hyperarousal or hypoarousal. If the magnitude of the stress is less than our capacity for dealing with stress, that is, it is within our window of tolerance, our stress-response system will do a good job of soothing and regulating the stress-induced changes in our body.

We commonly experience ebbs and flows in our stress levels. But we need to become aware of how big those fluctuations are and if they exceed the capacity of our stress-response system.

If our window of tolerance is tall, we have the capacity to absorb a large amount of stress before being thrown into a state of hyperarousal or hypoarousal, where we lose control of the ability to process and function well.

But if our window of tolerance is short, it does not take much to be thrown into a state of hyperarousal or hypoarousal and lose the ability to process and function well. Often, this is talked about as being triggered.

One situation where the effects of our window of tolerance can easily be seen is at an airport when a flight is delayed. Of course, every passenger experiences a different amount of stress depending on the consequences of the delay. It does not take much to notice which passengers are thrown outside their window of tolerance (I have been there) and which ones are able to stay within their window of tolerance.

When we go through trauma, the dissociation and disintegration we experience shrinks our window of tolerance. The unruly horse we spoke of earlier—our reptilian and mammalian brains—becomes more prone to bolt and enter into a state of hyperarousal or hypoarousal, causing the rider—our human brain—to have little ability to control or regulate the horse.

* * *

Van der Kolk summarizes the combined impact of these four dominoes falling well, writing, **"Trauma results in a fundamental reorganization of the way mind and brain manage perceptions. It changes not only how we think and what we think about, but also our very capacity to think."**

THE CONSEQUENCES OF TRAUMA ON OUR LEVEL OF VERTICAL DEVELOPMENT

Trauma and its common and predictable consequences trap us in the self-centered Mind 1.0 or Mind 2.0 levels, where our internal operating system is focused on protecting ourselves, either by keeping us safe, comfortable, and feeling like we belong, or by putting ourselves in a position where we can better control our situation and fill any inner voids through standing out, advancing, and getting ahead.

For me, learning about trauma and its common consequences has been life-changing in several ways. The first change was a shift away from judgment and criticism toward compassion and empathy, both toward others and myself.

In the past, when I saw someone doing something I did not agree with, my knee-jerk reaction was to essentially wonder, "What is wrong with them?" But now I am more inclined to wonder, "What happened to them?"

I am now also able to see more clearly the imprint of trauma on my life and ability to lead. I have come to see that all four dominoes of trauma have played a significant role throughout my adult life.

While I have only recently become aware of it, I have had an internal operating system that was oversensitive, causing me to possess self-protective mindsets that led me to misencode the world around me. I frequently saw safe things as being dangerous, which led to fear and limiting self-beliefs. This, in turn, held me back.

I also learned that, in certain situations, my window of tolerance was not as tall as I would have liked it to be. The situations where my window of tolerance was the shortest are connected to some childhood trauma. But more about that later.

We will now turn our attention to how these dominoes come together to influence our effectiveness as leaders. Ultimately, it is only by healing from our past trauma—including becoming more associated and integrated, improving our encoding processes, and widening our windows of tolerance—that we can develop vertically into Mind 3.0.

THE ROLE OF TRAUMA IN LEADERSHIP (IN)EFFECTIVENESS

When I work with organizations in helping them develop their leaders, three limitations most commonly surface: leaders' lack of self-awareness, their struggle to connect with and attune to those they lead, and their struggle to carry out their responsibilities effectively. These limitations are related to trauma and the four dominoes of trauma just discussed.

I recently attended a keynote address by Patrick Lencioni, the best-selling author of eleven books on leadership. Lencioni shared his experience working with the CEO of a well-known organization. He had just had the executive team rate the CEO on several leadership competencies. The results raised concerning findings, including a lack of openness to the ideas of those on his team and a lack of support.

Lencioni encouraged the CEO to be open with his executive team about the findings and share how he was going to take steps to improve. With some resistance, the CEO agreed to discuss the report in their next team meeting and invited Lencioni to observe and answer any questions, if need be.

During the meeting, Lencioni observed from the edge of the room. Report in hand, the CEO stood up and said, "This report says that I am close-minded and not open to others' ideas. What do you think?" He then asked each of his executive team members to state whether they agreed or disagreed with the report. As they went around, everyone disagreed with the statement.

The CEO continued, "This report says that I am not very supportive of you or your teams. What do you think?" Again, each of the executive team members vocally disagreed with the statement.

Lencioni told this story to help make the point that it is common for leaders to be unwilling to admit that they have weaknesses and mistakes. When we look through a trauma lens, we can see why this type of thinking and behavior is so common and why. As leaders, we are so often unwilling to be honest with ourselves and vulnerable with others.

Ultimately, trauma plays a foundational role in how effectively we relate to ourselves, others, and our work. Let us explore these three dynamics.

The Impact Trauma Has on How Leaders Relate to Themselves

Brain scans reveal that our body's response to trauma is to disactivate the self-sensing areas of the brain, including the medial prefrontal cortex, the anterior cingulate, the parietal cortex, and the insula. In other words, when we experience trauma and the first domino of dissociation falls, neurological changes occur.

What this means is that in order to cope with dread of trauma, we shut down the brain areas that transmit the visceral feelings and emotions that accompany and define terror. But in doing so, we are also shutting down the entire range of emotions and sensations that form the foundation of our self-awareness, our sense of who we are. So, in order to cope with trauma, we numb ourselves to make life tolerable.

Van der Kolk has found the price we pay for numbing is we "lose awareness of what is going on inside [our] body, and with that, the sense of being fully, sensually alive. . . . [We] become experts at ignoring [our] gut feelings and in numbing awareness of what is played out inside, [we] learn to hide from [ourselves]."

The effect is trauma prevents leaders from being self-aware. What makes this so challenging for those around us is this trauma-induced lack of self-awareness and the unwillingness to connect with our body leaves us in a state of denial. We are unable to see, let alone sit with, our flaws and weaknesses.

* * *

There are two ways I commonly see this lack of self-awareness show up in my consulting and coaching work.

The first is that it is not uncommon for a human resources leader to call me up and tell me they have a CEO that is wreaking havoc on the organization and the leadership team. By the time they call me, the CEO has typically kept HR from reaching out to a leadership coach, believing there is nothing wrong with their leadership and they do not need coaching.

This typically leads to HR shifting tactics. Knowing they cannot request coaching for the CEO, they ask me to do a series of workshops for the entire leadership team whom the CEO usually sees as not performing up to par. HR's hope is that by participating in a program for the whole leadership team, the CEO will get the support and guidance necessary for them to improve as a leader. When these engagements come to fruition, I commonly find, perhaps unsurprisingly, that the CEO is the most resistant to the development efforts.

The second way this lack of self-awareness shows up is when I walk leaders through a vertical development exercise designed to help them awaken to their self-protective self-sabotage. One step in the process involves asking the leader what fears might be driving some self-sabotaging behaviors we previously identified. For approximately 20 percent of leaders, the response I get is, "I don't have any fears. I am not driven by fear." They put up a wall of self-protection and become almost incapable of looking inward.

Both of these situations involve dissociative avoidance of leaders' inner workings, which plays out in the form of a lack of self-awareness. When leaders struggle to connect with themselves and explore whatever flaws or limitations they may possess, it is a clear signal they have experienced trauma at some time and it has yet to be addressed and healed.

What is going on with these leaders is they possess a subconscious belief that if they see or admit they have flaws or limitations, they will either feel worthless or like a failure. Thus, avoiding the exploration of their flaws or limitations is a self-protective defense mechanism that feels right to them but ultimately keeps them stuck. Such leaders continue to operate at a subpar level, believing it to be the best they can do, and they never grow and develop into a more positive force for good within their sphere of influence. Whenever I see a reluctance to turn inward, whether in myself or in others, I now view it as a signal that healing and vertical development are needed.

But the dominoes of trauma do not just limit our own growth and development, they also hinder our ability to effectively relate to and work with others.

The Impact Trauma Has on How Leaders Relate to Others

Dr. van der Kolk conducted a study to explore how parents who had experienced significant trauma in their lives interacted with their children. While this study involves the relationship between parent and child, I believe the phenomenon described also commonly occurs in the relationship between leaders and followers. He described his findings as follows:

> *Parents who are preoccupied with their own trauma, such as domestic abuse or rape or the recent death of a parent or sibling, may also be too emotionally unstable and inconsistent to offer much comfort and protection. While all parents need all the help they can get to help raise secure children, traumatized parents, in particular, need help to be attuned to their children's needs.*

Specifically, Van der Kolk found two patterns of interaction among the parents he observed. The first pattern involved parents who seemed too preoccupied with their own issues to attend to their children, even infants. These parents alternated between rejecting their children and acting as if they expected the child to respond to *their* needs as a parent. For example, Van der Kolk recalls a parent who came into his clinic and asked him for help with her two-month-old because the baby was "so selfish."

The second pattern involved parents who came across as sweet but did not know how to be the adult in the relationship. They seemed to want their children to comfort them. They struggled to greet their children after being away from them and did not pick their children up when they were distressed. But the mothers did not seem to be doing these things deliberately. They simply did not know how to be attuned to their children. As an example, Van der Kolk describes a video that is commonly used in therapist trainings:

> [This video features] a young mother playing with her three-month-old infant. Everything was going well until the baby pulled back and turned his head away, signaling that he needed a break. But the mother did not pick up on his cue, and she intensified her efforts to engage him by bringing her face closer to his and increasing the volume of her voice. When he recoiled even more, she kept bouncing and poking him. Finally, he started to scream, at which point the mother put him down and walked away, looking crestfallen.

What is interesting in this example is that the mother walked away from this situation feeling like the child did not love her. But the reality is very different. Because she was unable to accurately encode her child's initial cues, she engaged in well-intended behaviors that were essentially the opposite of what the child needed in that moment. In other words, she saw the baby as the problem while it was she who was the problem.

* * *

The dynamics associated with these two groups of parents are frequently seen in the workplace. It is incredibly common for leaders to be so concerned about their needs that they are unable to fully attune to the needs of their employees. Think about the primary focus of those in Mind 1.0 and Mind 2.0. Their focus is on themselves and fulfilling their needs. This keeps them from noticing the needs of those around them.

In Chapter Eleven, I mentioned how 75 percent of employees say their direct leader is the worst and most stressful part of their job and that 60 percent of employees report that their direct leader damages their self-esteem. With these statistics in mind, do you think these findings are driven by leaders who are out to get their employees? Of course not! These statistics are the result of leaders who, because of their past trauma, struggle to attune to those they lead.

When our mind is healthy and integrated, we readily resonate and attune to others. But if we are disintegrated, the two subsequent dominoes keep us from noticing the actions and emotions of others and appropriately responding to them.

First, we misencode. If we have had past experiences of being unseen, mistreated, or betrayed, we are more likely to be defensive, vigilant, and oversensitive, commonly feeling like others' actions are being directed against us.

Second, with a shrinking or small window of tolerance, we tend to become more reactive instead of receptive. We become less perceptive and understanding of the struggles, insecurities, and concerns of others, causing us to be harsher and less present with those we lead.

* * *

Let me give you an example of a leader I recently worked with who was able to awaken to his trauma-fueled misencoding and narrow window of tolerance.

Troy is a gregarious executive who admitted he commonly squashes his subordinates' ideas. As we probed this habit, he said he did not know why he did it; it was instinctual. To me, this was a clue that an operating system issue was driving him at a subconscious level.

As we unpacked this further, Troy concluded he squashed his subordinates' ideas because he was afraid that if those ideas were implemented, his teammates could be seen as being smarter than him.

Troy was seeing something good and safe—ideas for improvement—as being dangerous. This threw him outside of his narrow window of tolerance and led him to get defensive, a reaction that was automatic and unnecessary.

Troy finally came to realize his insecure need to be viewed as smart not only prevented him from seeing and caring about the perspectives and feelings of his subordinates, but it was causing him to be dominating and disengage his subordinates.

The Impact Trauma Has on Emotional Intelligence

When we put together how trauma impacts our ability to relate to ourselves and others, it leads us to an interesting discovery.

Emotional intelligence has been lauded as the most important factor for leadership effectiveness. Some research suggests that leaders' emotional intelligence is four times more important for leadership effectiveness than cognitive intelligence. As such, much has been written on this topic. Across all my reading and studying of emotional intelligence, though, I have never found a good explanation for what makes some people more emotionally intelligent than others.

Emotional intelligence has two components. The first is a self-awareness component, where we possess an ability to understand and manage our emotions. The second is an other-awareness component, where we possess an ability to understand and navigate the emotions of others.

By learning about the dominoes of trauma, it is easier to see that trauma is a significant inhibitor of emotional intelligence. Specifically, trauma research indicates when people are dissociated, they struggle to connect with and regulate their emotions. Dissociation inhibits self-awareness. And when people are disintegrated, prone to misencode, and have narrow windows of tolerance, they struggle to be sensitive to and effectively navigate others' emotions. Disintegration and its subsequent dominoes inhibit other-awareness.

This addresses a primary frustration I have when it comes to efforts to develop leaders' emotional intelligence. In my experience, whether observing or participating in such programs, the facilitators generally approach emotional intelligence as a horizontal development topic and primarily focus on helping people gain knowledge on the topic. If we are lucky, they might offer the chance to practice new skills, such as effective listening.

But emotional intelligence is not a horizontal development topic; it is a vertical development topic. Going through a training on how to listen more effectively is not likely to improve our emotional intelligence since it does not address dissociation and disintegration—the root causes of the lack of emotional intelligence.

Looking at emotional intelligence through the lens of trauma, I now understand why some people are more emotionally intelligent than others. This difference in emotional intelligence is foundationally rooted in the degree to which their mind has been affected by the dominoes of trauma.

The moral of the story is: **if we want to significantly improve the emotional intelligence of ourselves or others, we need to focus on healing the mind.**

The Impact Trauma Has on How Leaders Relate to Their Work

Dissociation, disintegration, misencoding, and narrow windows of tolerance not only impact how we navigate our social relationships, they also affect our ability to operate consistently at an effective level.

Earlier, we used the rider and the horse metaphor to make sense of how a disintegrated mind operates. When the path is smooth and easy, the rider—our human brain—is able to take charge. But if the horse—our reptilian and mammalian brains—gets spooked or the path gets difficult, the horse will bolt, and the rider is left holding on for dear life.

In light of this, we would do well to ask ourselves whether the path we, as leaders, are on is smooth and easy. It rarely is. More and more, we are having to operate in a setting that abounds in change, pressure, uncertainty, and complexity.

If we possess any of the four dominoes of trauma, it will be easy for us to feel challenged, surprised, or threatened in tumultuous environmental conditions, causing us to become more emotional and less regulated, logical, and present. This will play out in us being self-focused, having a shorter fuse, acting less mature, being overly defensive, and making poorer, short-sighted decisions.

In the heat of challenges, uncertainty, and complexity, the last thing we want is to cognitively and emotionally break down. Instead, we need to be fully present and have control of our cognitive and emotional resources. But this control will only come if we develop vertically and heal from our past trauma.

* * *

Remember Sharon? She was the head of development for a large tech company and could not sit still to take a call, was prone to dominating the settings she was in, was unwilling to acknowledge any of her flaws or weaknesses, micromanaged her team, and pushed them aside to get projects carried out as quickly as possible. She asked me to help her fix and speed up her leadership team.

Having learned about trauma and its consequences, it should be easy for you to see the fingerprints of trauma all over Sharon's leadership. Sharon has a high-strung nervous system that prevents her from being present. What's more, it limits her ability to be self-aware, causes her to be oversensitive to problems or slowdowns, and inhibits her from being attuned to the members of her leadership team.

What brought this home for me was one of our coaching calls, during which we had planned to do a vertical development exercise. The exercise requires the participant to be fully present.

Having worked with Sharon for a while by then, not much surprised me. When it came time for our Zoom call that morning, Sharon answered the video call while she was still at home, getting ready to head out to the office. She was running late and was stressed—her norm.

I asked her if she wanted to reschedule. She declined. So we started the call rather chaotically, with her running down the stairs, jumping into the car, and starting her commute. As always, she was talking fast, had her self-protective walls up, and was having a hard time being vulnerable.

Fortunately for me, Sharon got stuck in traffic. At first, she got agitated. But when it sunk in there was no way to get through the traffic jam, she resigned herself to connecting with me and the exercise. Sharon finally let her guard down, and we explored her self-sabotaging behaviors and the fears that were driving them. Ironically, while stuck in traffic, Sharon was the most open I had ever seen her.

As we reached the end of the introspective exercise, we paused to review the ground we had covered. I restated the fears Sharon had identified as being at the root of her less-than-ideal leadership style. For the most part, Sharon feared not being seen as valuable.

"Where does this fear come from?" I asked.

After a long, quiet minute, Sharon's eyes welled up with tears, and she said something that hit me at my core. "I chase after success because I don't have a good relationship with myself," she said. "I need the validation and recognition of others to make me feel good about myself."

Wow! What a vulnerable thing to say.

Her insight was eye-opening for both of us. I could not help but wonder where this lack of a positive relationship with herself came from. What trauma has she experienced throughout her life to feel this way?

Not long after, I read the following paragraph in *The Body Keeps the Score,* and I could not help but think of Sharon.

> It is one thing to process memories of trauma, but it is an entirely different matter to confront the inner void—the holes in the soul that result from not having been wanted, not having been seen, and not having been allowed to speak the truth. If your parents' faces never lit up when they looked at you, it's hard to know what it feels like to

be loved and cherished. If you come from an incomprehensible world filled with secrecy and fear, it's almost impossible to find the words to express what you have endured. If you grew up unwanted and ignored, it is a major challenge to develop a visceral sense of agency and self-worth.

Though Sharon and I did not dive into where her inner void came from, I do know this about her: Sharon's business is wildly successful. How she leads is chaotic and results-focused. She is clearly in Mind 2.0. But I also know Sharon has been through a messy divorce. She struggles to maintain a good relationship with her children. She has a hard time attuning to the needs of those around her. She has a hard time being self-aware. She has a narrow window of tolerance, such that when things get stressful, everyone in the office feels it.

I do not believe we should excuse Sharon's missteps and insensitivity. But when I try to understand her behavior, looking at her through the lens of trauma, I am much less inclined to be critical and much more inclined to be compassionate. I want her to heal from whatever wounds she has experienced. Until she does, she will continue to get in her own way.

The same is true for me and you. When we recognize that trauma causes us to make meaning of our world in less cognitively and emotionally sophisticated ways, we can see that vertical development, at its core, is about helping ourselves and others heal.

Knowing this, we can recognize that no amount of horizontal development will have a significant impact on the effectiveness of leaders like Sharon and ourselves.

MOVING TOWARD HEALING

Leaders affected by trauma generally do not engage in catastrophic negative behaviors. They make questionable decisions here and there. They communicate a little too brashly at times. They are unable to see complexity or handle stress well. They are not as sensitive as they should be to the feelings and psychological safety of those around them.

While none of these are fireable offenses, their implications add up, and they are still profound. When we work with trauma-affected leaders, it commonly feels like death by a thousand paper cuts.

This brings us to how we can help ourselves and others heal from trauma to become more positive influences in the world around us. To get a sense of where we are going, consider this quote by Bessel van der Kolk:

> *Trauma robs you of the feeling that you are in charge of yourself, of what I call self-leadership. . . . The challenge of recovery is to reestablish ownership of your body and your mind—of your self. This means feeling free to know what you know and to feel what you feel without becoming overwhelmed, enraged, ashamed, or collapsed. For most people this involves (1) finding a way to become calm and focused, (2) learning to maintain calm in response to images, thoughts, sounds, or physical sensations that remind you of the past, (3) finding a way to be fully alive in the present and engaged with the people around you, (4) not having to keep secrets from yourself, including secrets about the ways that you have managed to survive.*

If you would like to learn more about trauma and how it affects us, I offer a list of books at the end of Chapter Nineteen.

CHAPTER FOURTEEN

VERTICAL DEVELOPMENT: HEALING THE MIND

Vertical Development Law #14

Leaders put into place organizational structures, practices, and policies that emerge from their level of vertical altitude. More sophisticated leaders implement more sophisticated and effective structures, practices, and policies.

There are two primary objectives and two primary methodologies for healing from the effects of trauma. The two primary objectives are obvious when we know the dominoes of trauma:

- Overcome the dissociation that has occurred and create a greater association between mind and body.
- Address the disintegration that has occurred and create greater integration between the three major brain regions.

As for the methodologies for healing, there are top-down approaches, and there are bottom-up approaches.

TOP-DOWN AND BOTTOM-UP APPROACHES TO HEALING THE MIND

Top-down methodologies involve cognitive exercises and explorations that start at the highest level of our brain, our human brain, where cognition occurs. From there, we take a conscious and intentional dive down into the mammalian brain, reptilian brain, and then down into the body.

As we go through this process of cognitively connecting with ourselves, we help the body and mind reconnect through reassociation. In doing so, we start to integrate the wiring in our minds.

Cognitive behavioral therapy is one such top-down approach. In cognitive behavioral therapy, a person starts by identifying a situation they are struggling to navigate. Next, the therapist or coach will have their client identify the feelings that arise in their body as they talk through their thoughts, beliefs, and memories.

Top-down approaches require less assistance from others and are generally enough to help most leaders and people, particularly those whose trauma background is not too extreme.

For those whose trauma background is extreme, bottom-up approaches are generally the best place to start.

With bottom-up methodologies, we work in the opposite direction, starting with the feelings in the body and then connecting those to the nonconscious processes of our reptilian and mammalian brains and eventually to our human brain.

Since this approach does not start at a cognitive level, it is especially helpful to receive guidance and direction from a therapist. While both approaches are helpful on their own, healing can be accelerated if you combine the two.

With either approach, we become more settled and connected with ourselves. And as our mind becomes integrated, a proper balance between the three major brain regions is established, our encoding becomes more accurate, and our windows of tolerance expand.

When this occurs, we encode our lives more accurately. We experience greater control of ourselves and our lives. We become more centered and present. It takes more for our minds to get hijacked, allowing us to be more in charge of how we respond to and navigate our world.

We become empowered to be the proactive drivers of our life rather than simply being reactive passengers or the victims of our past.

MY EXPERIENCE HELPING LEADERS DEVELOP VERTICALLY

In my work with leaders, I focus primarily on top-down approaches that help leaders become conscious of aspects of themselves they have not been conscious of before, like their mindsets, fears, and self-limiting assumptions.

After creating conscious awareness in the human brain, I help clients move into the emotions and feelings held in the mammalian and reptilian brains. From there, we may even explore the sensations that occur in the body as we do this work.

In the next chapter, I will share more details on how we do this. For now, it is worth knowing how leaders commonly respond to this type of development.

I have been fortunate to do this work with hundreds of groups and thousands of leaders. As I have done so, an interesting pattern of responses has emerged. These range from excitement and enthusiasm to protective rage. Across this spectrum, I can broadly categorize leaders' responses to top-down vertical development in one of three ways.

The first response is a very positive one. It occurs in roughly 40 percent of leaders. These leaders are receptive to the content, willing to introspect about their mindsets and fears, and are able to sit with some discomfort as they deepen their self-awareness and identify aspects of themselves they may not be proud of. Although the work is not always enjoyable for them, they are inspired by it and are eager to continue working on their vertical development.

People who fall in this group tend to be in a healthy mental place where they are willing—even eager—to explore their flaws for the purpose of getting better. To empower this group of leaders to take developmental action on their mindsets, they simply need some clarity and direction.

I have found that by just putting labels on things, such as vertical development, integration, or growth mindset, these individuals are able to investigate where they currently are, see a more ideal place to be, and take action in that direction. By simply gaining insight and understanding, they become excited about taking further action to develop vertically.

The second response is more on the negative side, and it comes from another 40 percent of clients I work with. These leaders are cautiously optimistic about doing development work. When I first step into the room, I get the impression that they will engage if I can capture their attention and not ask too much of them. Generally, I find they do initially engage.

But once we start discussing their personal mindsets and fears, they physically stiffen, and emotionally, they become defensive and reluctant. It is uncomfortable for them to explore the idea that their beliefs, perspectives, and mindsets might be less than ideal. To them, it is a shot to their ego, and you can see the self-protection kick in.

This self-protection comes in different forms. Some leaders become quiet and disengaged. Other leaders get loud, and they seek to justify the beliefs, perspectives, or mindsets I may be pushing against.

I invite this dialogue because, for them to rewire their internal operating system, they need space to question and explore different higher-level beliefs, perspectives, and mindsets. While this group is generally not as keen as the first to engage and continue with the work of exploring mindsets and fears, I consider it a huge win when I get them to wrestle a little internally, push against preconceived beliefs and mindsets, and deepen their self-awareness.

Vertical development always starts with awareness. Thus, we have started this process for them. And when I come back to them weeks or months later, they commonly comment that thinking and being intentional about their mindsets has become something they do on a regular basis.

The final type of response is more actively negative. At least 20 percent of leaders I work with are openly resistant to the approach I take. When I invite them to explore their mindsets and fears, they put up a high wall.

Recently, I was contracted by a CEO to do some work with a board of directors for a nonprofit organization. A week before the event, the CEO called me up and said we needed to cancel the event. Apologetically, he explained that two board members were not happy with the results they got back from a mindset assessment I invited them to take, and they suggested they could use the time in a better way than talking about their mindsets. It made me chuckle that they were walking away from doing the inner work they probably needed most.

During workshops or coaching, I will also get comments like, "I don't have any fears." As you can tell, these leaders are even more vocal and opinionated in defending their position, beliefs, and related mindsets. Their strong defensiveness, to me, is a clear signal they have experienced something in their past they have not yet reconciled. These are the people who need vertical development the most, but they are the least likely to seek it out.

For the leaders in the second and third groups, the 60 percent who are either dismissive or resistant, I find it valuable to remind myself that their resistance is a form of self-protection that is rooted in trauma. Their resistance is a signal of the dominoes of trauma:

- They have a hard time introspecting and connecting with themselves: dissociation.
- Their reptilian and mammalian brains run a little too rampant: disintegration.
- They see development as being dangerous: misencoding.
- They are quick to be triggered and get defensive: narrow window of tolerance.

Having observed these varied responses to my vertical development efforts and knowing about the top-down and bottom-up approaches to healing, I have found different leaders need varying degrees of vertical development and healing help.

For the top 40 percent who are eager to engage in vertical development, the top-down approach that focuses on their mindsets is enough for them to make significant strides.

For the next 40 percent who are dismissive, the top-down approach that focuses on their mindsets is helpful, but in an ideal world, they would maximize value from supplemental bottom-up support.

For the 20 percent who are resistant, generally, the only way to help them is to start with a bottom-up approach. It is not until they can better connect with their bodies that they will be receptive to doing the introspective top-down approaches.

* * *

Over the next two chapters, we will carry on this conversation about top-down and bottom-up approaches to healing. In the next chapter, we will specifically look at a top-down approach I use in my consulting and coaching efforts. That approach centers on mindsets.

Before we get into this material, I invite you to take my mindset assessment. It is the most comprehensive and research-backed mindset assessment available. It will only take about five minutes to complete, after which you will receive your individualized results that indicate the quality of your mindsets as compared to the more than 25,000 others who have completed it.

You can complete the assessment by going to https://ryangottfredson. com/personal-mindset-assessment.

CHAPTER FIFTEEN

ELEVATING MINDSETS FOR VERTICAL DEVELOPMENT

Vertical Development Law #15
*The culture of an organization is a reflection of its leaders'
level of vertical development.*

Mindsets, or the long-range neural connections that are central to our meaning-making, are the linchpin of vertical development. Focusing directly on mindsets is the top-down approach that I use to help leaders develop vertically.

THREE PRIMARY STEPS TO IMPROVING OUR MINDSETS

Do you think improving our mindsets is easy, or is it difficult? What do you think?

To help answer that question and set the right expectations, let me ask another question: Is improving our mindsets generally the result of one grand event, or the result of doing a lot of little things repeatedly over time?

What you will see is that improving our mindsets is the result of doing a lot of little things repeatedly over time. Once you recognize this, the answer to the first question is that improving our mindsets is not necessarily easy, but it is generally not as difficult as most people think.

Improving our mindsets is not too different from learning how to count to ten in a different language. We first need to be motivated and believe it is possible for us to learn how to count to ten in a foreign language. Second, we need to learn the words associated with the numbers. Third, we need practice counting to ten in whatever language we chose. The same goes for improving our mindsets.

1. Having the Motivation and Belief that We Can Improve Our Mindsets

The first step in improving our mindsets involves developing the motivation to do so and believing it is possible.

I would imagine you are highly motivated to improve your mindsets. After all, you are nearing the end of a book describing the foundational role mindsets play in our vertical development and in becoming the leader and person we hope to be.

If you are someone tasked with fostering motivation in others to improve their mindsets, though, your role is to do what I have done: teach them about vertical development and the role mindsets play. This knowledge provides the reason why it is so important they become aware of the quality of their mindsets.

Do not hesitate to use my mindset assessment. It provides someone with objective data about the quality of their mindsets. My experience has taught me that most people think they have very positive mindsets. But across my database, I have found that only 2.5 percent are in the top quartile for the four sets of mindsets evaluated in the assessment. Having objectivity about the quality of their mindsets can help them awaken to the need to change and gain the motivation to embark on the journey to do so. Being motivated to change is not enough, though. They need to also believe they *can* change.

We have defined mindsets in several ways, including as mental lenses and encoding processes. Most of all, we defined them as neural connections that span our three major brain regions and integrate our brain such that the brain regions work together effectively. This description of mindsets being neural connections best illustrates the malleability of our mindsets.

Neuroscience has taught us neurons that fire together, wire together. This implies that mindsets are malleable, meaning they are consistently shifting and changing through the process of activating, firing, and wiring. Hence, the concept of neuroplasticity. Our mindset neural connections are no exception.

* * *

A research study showed how easy it is to activate more cognitively and emotionally sophisticated mindsets. The researchers randomly assigned participants to one of three groups.

The first group was told to write two paragraphs about their duties and responsibilities, a task designed to activate a negative, prevention mindset.

The second group was told to write two paragraphs about their goals and aspirations, a task designed to activate a positive, promotion mindset.

The third group did not engage in a journaling prompt. They were the control group.

Next, the researchers created teams of three with one person from each of these three groups. Each team was given a project to work on. While teams were working on the project, the researchers were measuring how active each team member was in the team's conversations.

After the team completed the project, each member was asked to choose one person from their group that they would like to work with again. What they found was individuals from group two, those who had written about their goals and aspirations, were significantly more likely to be active in their team's conversations and were voted as being the person their group members would most like to work with in the future.

This study demonstrates that small interventions to activate our mindsets can have significant short-term effects, causing us to process and behave in a manner that differs from our default processing mode.

Granted, a single intervention will not lead to lasting mindset improvements. But what if you were to engage in small exercises like this every day? Your positive mindsets would become stronger, and your mind would become more integrated, causing you to operate with greater cognitive and emotional sophistication.

2. Learning the Language of Mindsets

For most of us, our mindsets and internal operating system run below our level of consciousness. Whether for the positive or the negative, our mind automatically and nonconsciously assigns meaning to our experiences. This is why some of us naturally get defensive when we receive constructive criticism while others are naturally less reactive and more open to learning from constructive criticism.

One of the primary reasons why our mindsets lie below the level of our consciousness is because we have not developed a language for our mindsets. Without possessing labels, definitions, or descriptions, it is all but impossible to become aware and conscious of our mindsets. But the moment we put labels on different mindsets, define them, and describe them, we can bring them to the level of our consciousness and do something about them. You have got to name them to tame them.

When we learn about mindsets, we are empowering ourselves to consciously awaken to our previously nonconscious ways of operating. Using our consciousness to awaken to our nonconscious functioning is what classifies this vertical development approach as a top-down approach.

Keep in mind, the word *mindset* is used flippantly to describe our attitude toward something—entrepreneurial mindset, global mindset, money mindset, inclusive mindset, innovation mindset, and agile mindset, for example. These buzzwords are attractive, but they are limited in that they often lack a clear definition, and there is generally no research backing or supporting the notions associated with them. These are not the type of mindsets I am talking about in our vertical development journey.

In my review of the academic literature on mindsets, I have been able to identify four sets of mindsets that have been studied for thirty-plus years across the fields of psychology, education, management, and marketing. Because of the significant academic attention these mindsets have received, I feel more confident in their labels, descriptions, and validity.[1]

Each set of mindsets comes in pairs that represent polar ends of a continuum. On one side, you will find a mindset that is more self-protective, less cognitively and emotionally sophisticated, and leads to more limited processing and behaviors. As such, it leads to more negative outcomes. These are negative or limiting mindsets.

On the other side, you will find a mindset that is less self-protective, more cognitively and emotionally sophisticated, and leads to more optimal processing and behaviors. As such, it leads to more positive, value-creating outcomes. These are positive mindsets.

These sets are as follows:

NEGATIVE	POSITIVE
LIMITING	VALUE CREATING

Fixed............................Growth

Closed............................Open

Prevention....................Promotion

Inward............................Outward

Fixed and Growth Mindsets. Fixed and growth mindsets relate to how people make meaning of their ability to change and improve their talents, abilities, and intelligence.

---

1   If you would like greater depth on any of these sets of mindsets, you might like my book, *Success Mindsets: Your Keys to Unlocking Greater Success in Your Life, Work, & Leadership*, a *Wall Street Journal* and *USA Today* best-seller.

When someone has a **fixed mindset**, they do not believe they or others can change or improve their talents, abilities, and intelligence. They tend to think they are who they are and there is nothing they can do about it. Who they are now is the same person they were five years ago, and who they will be five years from now is the same person they are now.

When people have a fixed mindset, they tend to see the world in terms of haves and have-nots. If something does not come naturally or quickly to them or if they fail, they see this as a signal that they are a have-not, and because they do not believe they can change their talents, abilities, and intelligence, they do not believe they can become a "have."

Thus, those with a fixed mindset are generally concerned about struggling or failing. They do not want to look bad or be seen as a have-not. Or, to phrase this more positively, those with a fixed mindset are generally concerned about looking good. They always want to put their best foot forward, and they are reluctant to try new or difficult things they are not sure they will be successful at. They are inclined to self-protect their image and appearance.

When someone has a **growth mindset**, they believe they and others can change and improve their talents, abilities, and intelligence. They tend to think they are a very different person than who they were five years ago, and they are only a shadow of who they will be five years from now.

Those with a growth mindset do not see the world in terms of haves and have-nots. If something does not come naturally or quickly to them or if they fail, that may mean they are a have-not right now, but because they believe they can change their talents, abilities, and intelligence, this does not preclude them from becoming a have in the future.

As a result, those with a growth mindset are not overly concerned about avoiding failure, looking bad, or protecting their image. This allows them to focus on learning and growing, embracing challenges, and persisting even if something does not come naturally to them.

* * *

Your mindset assessment results should give you a sense of the quality of your mindset along this fixed-to-growth continuum.

I have all sorts of people who take my mindset assessment. One thing I have observed is that out of the four sets of mindsets, business leaders and executives struggle with this set the most. Surprisingly, they are generally more fixed-minded than growth-minded. This may be because business leaders feel a lot of social pressure to always look good and never fail, which could incentivize them to take on more of a fixed mindset.

This might be justifiable. Most of us do not like to look bad or fail. But if we have a fixed mindset and our internal operating system is wired to avoid failure so we can look good, where is our focus? It is on ourselves. We are being self-protective, either because of the Mind 1.0 needs to stay safe, comfortable, and belong, or because of the Mind 2.0 needs to stand out, advance, and get ahead.

On the other hand, if we possess a growth mindset, we are in a centered mental space where our window of tolerance is wider. We have the cognitive and emotional sophistication to recognize that

- failing and looking bad are not inherently dangerous;
- we learn, grow, and develop the most when we fail or look bad; and
- the more we learn, grow, and develop, the more we can fulfill our Mind 3.0 needs for contributing, adding value, and lifting those we work with and serve.

* * *

To fully appreciate the cognitive and emotional sophistication and benefits of a growth mindset over a fixed mindset, consider the role they play in how we approach learning challenges.

As we navigate through life, we will encounter situations where there are invitations to try something new. These situations vary in their level of difficulty and can be categorized as **comfort zone challenges, performance zone challenges,** and **learning zone challenges**.

To fully grasp the way our mindsets influence how we take on challenges of varying difficulties, create a mental image. Envision a plateau on both the left and right sides of the image with a pit in the middle. The left plateau represents where you are, including your current development and skill levels. The pit represents the idea that if we take on this new challenge, we will be stepping into a space of uncertainty. The height of the right plateau represents how difficult the challenge is relative to your current development and skill levels.

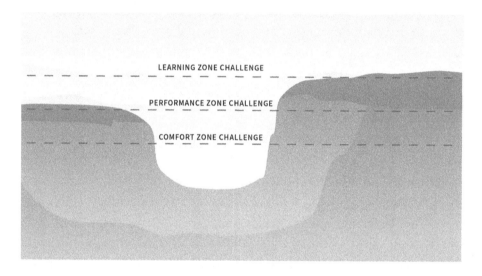

LEARNING ZONE CHALLENGE

PERFORMANCE ZONE CHALLENGE

COMFORT ZONE CHALLENGE

All of our challenges are new experiences, but a **comfort zone challenge** is one that we are quite confident we can master given our current development and skill levels. Visually, this can be depicted as the plateau on the right being lower than the plateau on the left. Given we have already climbed to a certain elevation and the elevation associated with the challenge is lower, we feel confident that we can drop down into the pit and climb back out on the other side without much difficulty.

A **performance zone challenge** occurs when the challenge is equal to our current development and skill levels. Visually, the plateaus on either side of the image are equal in height. The challenge will require us to use the fullness of our development and skill levels in order to master it.

In these situations, we generally feel some anxiety about our ability when dropping into the pit because we know that getting up the other side will be challenging. But these challenges can be fun because they push us to our current limits.

A **learning zone challenge** occurs when the challenge is greater than our current development and skill levels. Visually, the plateau on the right is taller than the plateau on the left. What this means is the challenge exceeds our current limits.

If we choose to take on the challenge and drop into the pit, it is rather unlikely we will be able to climb out on our first attempt. We will likely fail and fall back into the pit at some point during our climb.

Having either a fixed or growth mindset dictates which challenges we are willing to take on. They also play a role in our subsequent growth and development.

When we have a **fixed mindset**, we will eagerly take on comfort zone challenges. These are easy ways for us to demonstrate our talent and look good. We will generally only take on performance zone challenges if we are certain that we can get up on the other side without failure or looking bad. And we generally avoid learning zone challenges because we inherently believe that if we try and fail, we will be seen as a failure.

When we have a **growth mindset**, on the other hand, we are willing to approach all three types of challenges. In particular, we take a much more positive outlook toward the learning zone challenges. We recognize that we may not be successful on our first try, but we know with continued effort, we can conquer the challenge and end up at a higher elevation.

* * *

Closed and Open Mindsets. Closed and open mindsets are related to how open we are to the ideas and suggestions of others.

Why would anyone ever possess a **closed mindset**, where they are closed to the ideas and suggestions of others? At a foundational level, it is because they believe what they know is best. They see their mind as a bucket, and their bucket is full. What happens if you try to pour something into a full bucket? It simply overflows.

Brené Brown describes always having to be right—something she calls having to be "the knower"—as a form of defensiveness. She says, "For many people, the need to be a knower is driven by shame and, for some, even trauma. Being the knower can save people in hard situations, and it's easy to buy into the belief that being a knower is the only value we bring to relationships and work."

When we believe what we know is best, we become focused on being right or being seen as right. We want to be the ones providing answers, and because we are not asking questions, we do not allow space for new or different perspectives.

If we look beneath the hood, so to speak, we will either find a Mind 1.0 internal operating system that is programmed to hold onto our ideas and perspectives as a way to stay safe and/or fit in with our tribe, or we will find a Mind 2.0 internal operating system that is programmed to vocalize and promote our ideas and perspectives as a way to stand out and be recognized.

Generally, when we are in Mind 1.0 or Mind 2.0, we have a hard time admitting we have been wrong and dislike having our ideas challenged. We see these things as threats to standing in or standing out.

When we have an **open mindset**, we believe we can be wrong. While we might have a lot of knowledge and expertise in our bucket, we leave some room for the idea that we can be wrong. We do not care about being right, we care about finding truth and thinking optimally. With a desire to find truth and think optimally, we are much more inclined to ask questions and to seek out new and different perspectives. Also, we are much more willing to rethink and unlearn. Thus, with an open mindset, we can absorb new ideas and suggestions.

If we look beneath the hood of an open-minded person, we will find an internal operating system that cares little about fitting in with the ideas of their tribe and using their ideas to stand out or get ahead. Instead, we will find a Mind 3.0 internal operating system that is programmed to adopt the ideas and suggestions that will help them better contribute, add value, and lift those they work with and serve. They have the cognitive and emotional sophistication to be okay admitting they have been wrong and to have their ideas challenged so they can refine their thinking.

Your personal mindset results should help you awaken to the degree to which you possess a closed or open mindset and help you get a better sense of your internal operating system as it relates to new ideas and different perspectives.

* * *

Prevention and Promotion Mindsets. Prevention and promotion mindsets are related to how we approach life. Do we approach life with a focus on avoiding problems, or do we approach life with a focus on reaching goals?

I have seen statistics that indicate that 83 percent of people do not have set goals, and only 3 percent of Americans have written goals. When we do not have goals or a clear destination that we are heading toward, it is easy to default to a **prevention mindset**, where we become primarily focused on avoiding problems and ensuring our comfort and enjoyment.

When we do have goals and a clear destination that we are heading toward, we are more inclined to have a **promotion mindset**, where we become primarily focused on accomplishing our goals, even if it means wading through problems or being uncomfortable for part of our journey.

To make these mindsets come to life, imagine two ship captains, one with a prevention mindset and the other with a promotion mindset.

A prevention-minded ship captain's number-one focus is on not sinking. That captain does not want any problems to occur. He does not want to take any risks, nor does he want to rock the boat. With this mentality, how is the prevention-minded ship captain likely to respond to a storm heading in the ship's direction? He will likely run from the storm and go to a place that is safe and comfortable, like a harbor, where he can wait out the storm. But is that harbor the destination he originally set out for? Unlikely!

A promotion-minded ship captain, of course, does not want his ship to sink. But his number-one focus is on making progress toward their destination. With this mentality, how will he likely respond to a storm heading in his direction? He will ask, "Does this storm stand between where I am and where I want to go?"

If the answer is yes, he will not run from the storm. Instead, he will prepare to take on the storm, batten down the hatches, and muster up the courage to brave the challenges associated with the storm. A promotion-minded captain will be willing to do this because he knows it is the only way he will be able to get to the destination.

When we have a **prevention mindset**, we primarily focus on playing it safe and staying comfortable. This is very much a Mind 1.0 mentality. A **promotion mindset**, though, can be either a Mind 2.0 mentality or a Mind 3.0 mentality—it just depends on our focus within the promotion mindset. Are we focused on making progress toward our destination so we can stand out, or are we focused on making progress toward our destination because we recognize those we are serving will be better off at that destination?

The mindset assessment you took will give you a sense of where you are on the continuum between prevention and promotion mindsets. If you have a promotion mindset, it will not do a very good job of identifying whether you have a Mind 2.0 promotion mindset or a Mind 3.0 promotion mindset. It will be up to you to do some introspection and determine your motivation. Do you want to reach your destination to stand out or to create value?

* * *

Inward and Outward Mindsets. Inward and outward mindsets are related to the value we place on others relative to the value we place on ourselves.

Think of a time when someone passed you while driving—whether on a freeway or while trying to exit an event—and then turned on their blinker to merge into your lane in front of you. Have you ever prevented them from merging? I know I am not the only one guilty of having done this. At the end of the day, not allowing someone in is not that big of a deal, but it can be rude.

When we refuse to let people cut in, we are telling ourselves that our spot in this lane is more important to us than it is to the other driver. After preventing them from merging, we may feel a need to justify being a jerk. We do not say, "I didn't let that *person* in." What we say is, "I didn't let that *car* in."

Taking this stance, we are elevating our needs above the needs of others, and to feel okay about doing this, we dehumanize the other people involved, seeing them more like an object than a person.

This is what it looks like when we have an **inward mindset**: we see ourselves as being more important than others. As a result, we tend to see others as objects, possibly as obstacles in our way or as instruments to help us get where we are going.

But when we have an **outward mindset**, we see others as being just as important as ourselves. As a result, we see them as people and value them.

I venture to say that at the root of all human atrocities is an inward mindset.

Recall our discussion about those in Mind 1.0 and Mind 2.0 relative to those in Mind 3.0. What is our primary focus in Mind 1.0 and 2.0? It is an inward focus on ourselves, whether on standing in or standing out. As such, when we are in Mind 1.0 and 2.0, our internal operating system is programmed with an inward mindset.

Where is our focus when we are in Mind 3.0, though? It is on our contribution, adding value, and lifting others. This is inherently outward. The only way we can be here is if we see others as being as important, if not more important, than ourselves.

The Four Sets of Mindsets. The purpose of identifying, labeling, and describing these four sets of mindsets is to help you learn the language of mindsets. To put a cap on these descriptions, let me take you through an exercise my clients find helpful.

Listed below are four desires. These are to:

- Look good
- Be right
- Avoid problems
- Get ahead

Does society suggest these desires are good or bad? Think about it.

My perception is that society suggests these desires are all good. This is because no one desires to look bad, be wrong, have problems, or get passed up.

So, the four desires feel justifiable, if not good. But when we have these desires, where is our focus? On ourselves. They are fueled by the limiting mindsets: fixed, closed, prevention, and inward.

While the desires may be justifiable, they are not cognitively and emotionally sophisticated. They are Mind 1.0 and Mind 2.0 perspectives.

More positive desires that are fueled by the positive mindsets are to:

- Learn and grow (growth)
- Find truth and think optimally (open)
- Reach goals (promotion)
- Lift others (outward)

When we have these desires, our focus is not on our self-protection or self-advancement, it is on contributing, the focus of those who operate in Mind 3.0. Not only are these desires more cognitively and emotionally sophisticated, but it takes elevating our cognitive and emotional sophistication to adopt these desires and associated mindsets. Specifically:

- To learn and grow, we must be okay with looking bad at times.
- To find truth and think optimally, we must be okay with being wrong at times.
- To reach goals, we must be okay with wading through problems at times.
- To lift others, we must be okay with putting ourselves on the back burner at times.

To be okay with looking bad, being wrong, wading through problems, and putting ourselves on the back burner is not easy, especially in the moment. It requires developing a wide window of tolerance for each of these things. Once we have that wide window of tolerance and are willing to look bad, be wrong, wade through problems, and put ourselves on the back burner *at times*, it is evidence that we are operating from a high vertical altitude.

3. Exercising Our Positive Mindset Neural Connections

Once we learn the language of mindsets, the next step is to exercise, activate, and strengthen our positive mindsets. How to do this becomes clear when we remember that our mindsets are neural connections, and neural connections that fire together, wire together. In other words, the more we use certain neural connections, the stronger they become.

The reality is that we all have fixed *and* growth neural connections, closed *and* open neural connections, prevention *and* promotion neural connections, and inward *and* outward neural connections. Of these pairs, one of the neural connections is typically stronger than the other. And when one is stronger than the other, it fires more rapidly and more readily, serving as the default neural connection that filters and processes information.

When we have a limiting mindset neural connection that is stronger than a positive mindset neural connection, this means through our life, we have used and relied upon that limiting mindset neural connection more than our positive mindset neural connection. The reason for this is likely connected to trauma. In fact, we can interpret our limiting mindsets as maladaptive stress responses to past experiences.

Each of the limiting mindsets causes us to be oversensitive to potential threats (looking bad, being wrong, having problems, and getting passed up) and overly self-protective so we can meet our needs (looking good, being right, avoiding problems, and getting ahead).

If we want to create top-down healing and integration in our mind, we need to consciously and routinely activate and strengthen our positive mindsets. Effectively, we need to hit the gym for our brain.

Comparing our neural connections to muscles again, if we want to strengthen our muscles, we do not only go to the gym once. We have to work out regularly. At first, we need to be highly intentional about this. But over time, it becomes a habit and a part of our routine. The more we go and the harder we push ourselves, the stronger and bigger our muscles will become. The same is true for our mindsets.

* * *

There was a fascinating study done where researchers took a group of financial professionals who were stressed out and divided them into two groups. They showed one group a three-minute video about how stress is debilitating. This induced a stress-is-bad mindset. Meanwhile, they showed the other group a three-minute video about how stress is enhancing, thereby inducing a stress-is-good mindset.

Two weeks later, they measured the participants' engagement, performance, and blood pressure. Those who watched the stress-is-enhancing video had higher engagement, higher performance, and lower blood pressure than their colleagues who watched the stress-is-debilitating video.

Watching a single three-minute video—that is, doing a single mindset workout—had a significant impact on how individuals thought about their work, how they behaved at work, and even how healthily their bodies functioned.

While this single workout may have had positive effects for a couple of weeks, we cannot expect that watching just one video will lead to a permanent change in our engagement, performance, and blood pressure.

What if we were to stack interventions like this on top of each other, such that we spend a few minutes every day activating and strengthening our positive mindset neural connections? Over a short period, our limiting mindsets would atrophy, and our positive mindsets would become the dominant way of processing our world.

When our positive mindsets become stronger than our limiting mindsets, this is evidence that neural healing has occurred and our mind is more integrated than it had been. The benefit of this improved integration is we will encode our world more accurately and expand our window of tolerance.

EXERCISES FOR YOUR POSITIVE MINDSET NEURAL CONNECTIONS

Fortunately, there have been more than thirty years of research on all four sets of mindsets that provide us with empirical evidence about what exercises are effective in activating and strengthening our positive mindsets. The most effective exercises include the following:

- Reading books and articles about growth mindsets, open mindsets, promotion mindsets, and outward mindsets
- Watching videos that promote the activation of the positive mindsets
- Journaling
- Having discussions with others who are interested in changing their mindsets
- Becoming aware of and improving your self-talk

I have integrated all these resources into my Digital Vertical Development Coach, available to you for free from Qstream. Thus, if you would like to streamline the process of exercising your mindsets, this is for you. Again, you can get this at www.Qstream.com/TheElevatedLeader.

In addition, you can find a Mindset Development Planning Guide and a host of resources at www.ryangottfredson.com/vertical-development-resources.

Summary of a Mindset-Focused, Top-Down Approach

For many, the idea of shifting and improving our mindsets feels daunting initially. While it may not be easy, it is much easier than you may have thought.

Referring to a top-down approach like what I have described, Dr. van der Kolk suggests the following about emotions, and the same can also be said of mindsets: "Change begins when we learn to 'own' our emotional brains. That means learning to observe and tolerate the . . . sensations that register misery and humiliation. Only after learning to bear what is going on inside can we start to befriend, rather than obliterate, the emotions that keep our maps fixed and immutable."

Putting labels on our mindsets and being cognizant of them makes it easier to own and change them.

This top-down approach to healing our minds seems to be sufficient for most leaders to make significant strides in their vertical development. But there is a large enough percentage who have a hard time being introspective and evaluating their internal operating system. Before they can do this top-down work, they need to create a healthier association between their mind and body. This is the focus of the next chapter: bottom-up approaches to healing from our trauma and elevating our ability to lead effectively.

CHAPTER SIXTEEN

BOTTOM-UP APPROACHES FOR VERTICAL DEVELOPMENT

Vertical Development Law #16
Organizations cannot evolve beyond their leaders' level of vertical development.

If we were to ask a hundred random people if they possessed a good mind–body connection, I believe they would all say, "Yes, I have a good mind–body connection."

This can be misleading, and we may be misleading ourselves. What is misleading is that across those hundred individuals, we will find large variability in the degree to which their minds and bodies are connected. Some will have a strong connection, and others will have a rather weak connection. Regardless of the quality of your mind–body connection, I believe we all *think* we have a good sense of what's going on in our bodies.

The challenge is that very few people have a great mind–body connection. They have never experienced or felt what a great mind–body connection feels like. Yes, we all have some degree of a mind–body connection, but because we have not experienced a better connection, it is hard to be objective about it.

In a way, this is similar to being color-blind. Unless someone who is color-blind purchases special glasses to see the full spectrum of colors, they will think their eyesight is good enough and will never know what they are missing out on.

You may be experiencing the same phenomenon. You may think your mind–body connection is good enough, yet not know what you are missing out on.

For me, I never had any reason to question my mind–body connection, and I assumed the connection I had was good. But as I studied the effects and consequences of trauma and investigated my own, I learned that I have spent most of my life without a great mind–body connection, which has held me back from experiencing life fully. I have only recently started to work on improving my mind–body connection, and I have found the experience eye-opening.

Having a weakened mind–body connection is not uncommon. It is the result of the first domino of trauma: dissociation.

In *The Body Keeps the Score*, Van der Kolk expresses how common dissociation is and how profound it can be. (Allow me to add here that I rely heavily on insights from Dr. van der Kolk's work in this chapter as his expertise lies in resolving trauma and helping people strengthen their mind–body connection.) He writes:

> *I was amazed to discover how many of my patients told me they could not feel whole areas of their bodies. Sometimes I'd ask them to close their eyes and tell me what I had put into their outstretched hands. Whether it was a car key, or a can opener, they often could not even guess what they were holding—their sensory perceptions simply weren't working.*

As problematic as it might be to not be able to engage fully in sensory experiences, these are not the only effects of dissociation. More problematic is the fact that, as Van der Kolk writes, "When our senses become muffled, we no longer feel fully alive."

Our inability to recognize we might not have a great connection to our body, while believing we do, is a primary reason why top-down approaches do not work for everyone. If someone is unwilling to explore how their limiting mindsets are holding them back from living life at a higher and more effective level, they will continue seeing life through suboptimal lenses with no desire to change. They simply do not see why they need to change.

This inability to notice the limiting lenses through which they see life is why bottom-up approaches can be so helpful. The goal of bottom-up approaches is to strengthen the mind–body connection that may have been damaged or disrupted because of dissociation.

Such approaches begin as far away from our resistant conscious processing as possible. They start with a focus on connecting with our body, then move upward to explore the feelings that arise within our reptilian and mammalian brains, after which we can make sense of those feelings using our human brain.

Methodically exploring these connections in a bottom-up fashion helps to create a healthy association between the mind and body, enabling us to engage in our world with a richer sensory and emotional experience as we live our lives. It helps us to see in full color as opposed to muted color.

"Trauma robs you of the feeling that you are in charge of yourself," Van der Kolk writes. Through a bottom-up approach to the healing of the mind, we can once again establish ownership of our body and mind, of our very self. In the process of healing, you become "free to know what you know and to feel what you feel without becoming overwhelmed, enraged, ashamed, or collapsed."

Gaining this freedom, Van der Kolk explains,

> . . . involves (1) finding a way to become calm and focused, (2) learning to maintain calm in response to images, thoughts, sounds, or physical sensations that remind you of the past, (3) finding a way to be fully alive in the present and engaged with the people around you,

(4) not having to keep secrets from yourself, including secrets about the ways that you have managed to survive.

INTEROCEPTION

The technical term for the mind–body connection that has been described is called interoception. Commonly referred to as our body's sixth sense, it is our ability to sense what is going on in our body.

Whether we have experienced the dissociative effects of trauma or not, we all have interoceptive abilities. Such abilities primarily revolve around our physical regulation. But it can also help us regulate our emotions.

We feel hungry when we need nutrients. We feel thirsty when we need hydration. We feel like we need to go to the bathroom when our body needs to dispose of waste. And we also feel fatigued when we are tired. All of these sensations are designed to help us physically regulate.

If we have experienced the dissociative effects of trauma, though, our interoceptive abilities may be weaker than those of others who have experienced less dissociative effects of trauma.

When someone has weak interoceptive abilities, their interoceptive abilities are still present, but they are muted. Trauma experts have found that people who have experienced more trauma are less receptive to their body's signals of hunger, thirst, or fatigue. And as seen in the opening quote by Van der Kolk, some folks who have a greater history of trauma can even be less receptive to touch, losing some of their ability to figure out what object was placed in their hand.

Strengthening our interoceptive abilities is a critical part of trauma healing. Van der Kolk states:

> *Trauma victims cannot recover until they become familiar with and befriend the sensations in their bodies. Being frightened means that you live in a body that is always on guard. Angry people live in angry bodies. The bodies of child-abuse victims are tense and defensive until they find a way to relax and feel safe. In order to change, people need to become aware of their sensations and the way that their bodies*

interact with the world around them. Physical self-awareness is the first step in releasing the tyranny of the past.

The first step to connecting with our body is to become aware of the feelings within it. While it seems obvious from the outside that angry people live in angry bodies, defensive people live in defensive bodies, and sad people live in sad bodies, most people who live in these bodies cannot sense that they are any more angry, defensive, or sad than others.

Strengthening Our Interoceptive Abilities

To strengthen our interoceptive abilities, we need to practice noticing and describing the feelings in our bodies. Dr. van der Kolk describes his process as helping patients "notice then describe the feelings in their bodies." Rather than describe the emotions themselves, he has them identify "the physical sensations beneath the emotions: pressure, heat, muscular tension, tingling, caving in, feeling hollow, and so on."

He also helps patients "become aware of their breath, their gestures and movements," and invites them "to pay attention to subtle shifts in their bodies, such as tightness in their chests or gnawing in their bellies, when they talk about negative events that they claim did not bother them."

These bottom-up meditative approaches related to trauma healing are based on a few assumptions:

- Trauma causes unbearable feelings and sensations.
- Even though dissociation cuts off our ability to feel these unbearable feelings and sensations, the unbearable feelings and sensations are still held in our body.
- Continuing to avoid feeling these sensations increases our vulnerability to being overwhelmed by them. Whether we can recognize it or not, ignored trauma-related feelings and sensations leave us trapped, constraining us in Mind 1.0 or Mind 2.0 programming focused on and oversensitive about our safety, comfort, and belonging, or our standing out, advancing, and getting ahead. As

long as we keep our distance from these feelings and sensations, they will continue to boil beneath our conscious awareness.

- While it is not easy to connect with the trauma-related feelings and sensations, it is only when we connect with them that we can do something about them. If we can get more in touch with our inner world, noticing our fear, nervousness, or anxiety, we can gain control over it.

Because connecting with our bodies might be new for us and possibly distressing, I believe it is best for us to have a therapist or a trained professional to help guide us in most of the bottom-up healing we might do. If you were to engage in bottom-up approaches with a therapist or trained professional, let me provide an overview of some of the things you might do.

Meditation. This is a practice of awareness. There are many forms and objectives of meditation, including top-down and bottom-up meditative practices.

The top-down approaches focus more on consciously regulating our body's stress-response system. This can be helpful and healing. But again, the connection between our mind and our body might be so bad that we are inclined to avoid exploring this connection in a top-down conscious fashion.

Bottom-up meditations are practices and exercises where we allow ourselves to sit with and explore our bodies. Commonly, this is done in the form of a body scan. In guided body-scan meditations, we are guided to pay attention to different parts of our body and recognize whether there are any feelings or tension in different areas.

In my personal practice, I generally feel quite relaxed when I begin my meditations. But, interestingly, as I scan my body, I become aware I am contracting certain muscle groups, completely oblivious to the tension I am holding.

Bottom-up meditations are a safe way for us to start reestablishing and strengthening our mind–body connection.

Body Connection Activities. When we are in a state of dissociation and have to confront a stressful situation, we commonly respond to that stress, not by noticing, naming, and sitting with it, but by ignoring or running from it. When we do this, we are suppressing our body's inner cries, and these commonly show up later as sleeplessness, migraines, asthma attacks, and illness.

In order to expand our ability to more fully engage with uncomfortable feelings rather than run from them, therapists often recommend various body connection activities that require the participant to spend quality time consciously connecting with their body's positioning and feelings. Such activities include therapeutic massage or other touch therapies, kickboxing, yoga, Pilates, and even equine therapy.

Therapy. Just as there are therapy modalities that utilize a top-down approach (cognitive behavioral therapy, for example), there are therapy modalities that utilize a bottom-up approach. I have experienced the benefits of two of these: eye-movement desensitization and reprocessing (EMDR) and internal family systems (IFS) therapy.

EMDR. EMDR is increasingly found to be one of the most effective therapeutic approaches to treating trauma. The eye movement reference comes from the early days of EMDR where, when exploring one's traumatic past, the therapist would hold up a finger and move it back and forth. The patient would follow the finger with his or her eyes.

Today, therapists use a variety of lateral stimuli that include fingers moving back and forth, moving dots on a screen, tapping one's shoulders back and forth, or audio pings going back and forth. For reasons scientists do not fully understand, engaging in this lateral stimulation allows people to revisit their past trauma while staying within their window of tolerance.

This is when the desensitizing and reprocessing part of EMDR comes in. While staying within their window of tolerance, the therapist can guide the patient in becoming desensitized to their past trauma and reprocessing that trauma in healthier ways.

IFS Therapy. This therapy operates on the assumption that individuals have an internal community or family of subpersonalities—also referred to as *parts*—that have different goals and motivations, along with different levels of maturity, excitability, wisdom, and pain.

IFS therapy is all about getting to know these parts, making sure they are taken care of, and helping them to heal so they do not sabotage each other or cause us to sabotage ourselves. It has proven helpful for treating trauma-related issues that include compulsive behaviors, eating disorders, depression, anxiety, and bipolar disorders.

* * *

When I began doing EMDR with my therapist, I was unaware she was going to engage in IFS as well. And had I known she was, I think I would have resisted doing it. I did not think there were different parts to myself. But as we started to dive into challenging parts of my past and I explored the feelings in my body, I discovered that I indeed had different parts within me that were performing different self-protective roles.

This amazed me, not only because I actually discovered parts of myself I had not been aware of, but because of how clear they felt in terms of where they resided in my body, the role they played, and the feelings they carried.

One part resides in my upper-left chest and plays the role of energizer. It fuels my passions and gives energy to my body. To me, there was significance in its proximity to my heart. Another part resides in the lower part of my chest, where my diaphragm is. This part operates as the protector of my emotions.

We also identified a part of me being protected by my protector. In IFS therapy, this is called an *exile*, a part of ourselves connected to past trauma that we tend to keep hidden. While the exile likes being protected by my protector, its wanting to hide has left it alone and scared. By identifying this part, I have been able to give it love and attention. Doing this has felt incredibly healing, and I feel like I have a better and more secure relationship with myself.

THE HEALING POWER OF BOTTOM-UP APPROACHES

Our body is amazing and can do many incredible things. Without any conscious thought, our heart beats about 100,000 times per day, our lungs take in oxygen about 20,000 times per day, and our digestive system turns food into energy.

And as we have discussed, when we experience trauma, our body goes to extreme measures to keep us alive. Unfortunately, the reality is that during such traumatic situations, our body is focused on winning the immediate battle and not the long-term war.

The numbing associated with dissociation may allow us to live on despite experiencing horrors, but the lingering dissociation results in decreased interoceptive abilities.

Lightbulbs and Mind Levels

Our interoceptive abilities are a lot like an electric circuit and a light bulb. For a lightbulb to work, it needs to be connected to a source of electricity, and the strength of the electric current must be strong enough to power the lightbulb. When the current is weak, the lightbulb burns dimly. When the current is strong, the lightbulb burns brightly.

The strength of our interoceptive abilities, that is, the connection between our body and mind, is not unlike the strength of the electric current in a circuit. The less connected our mind is to our body, the more dimly we operate. And the more connected our mind is to our body, the more brightly we operate.

From a vertical development perspective, trauma-induced dissociation commonly restrains us at the Mind 1.0 level. In this damaged and self-protecting condition, our internal operating system focuses on ensuring our safety, comfort, and belonging. But dissociation still exists at the Mind 2.0 level, where we seek after standing out, advancing, and getting ahead to fill a dissociative void.

At either of these mind levels, we are inclined to think our interoceptive abilities are strong or, at least, strong enough. We can tell there is some level of connection between our mind and body. The lightbulb is on, if you will. But what we generally have a difficult time recognizing is how brightly our bulb is burning.

This analogy implies that if we want to be a brighter light in our world, we need to improve our interoceptive abilities and strengthen the connection and relationship between our mind and body.

The more we connect with our body and its feelings, the less we need to focus on either the Mind 1.0 needs for safety, comfort, and belonging or the Mind 2.0 needs for standing out, advancing, and getting ahead, and the more we can focus on the Mind 3.0 needs for contributing, adding value, and lifting others.

While top-down approaches can certainly help with fostering greater association between mind and body, many of us find it challenging to consciously connect with our body through our human brain. This is due to dissociation and disintegration that short-circuits the messaging between our mind and our body. It is only when we connect with our body first that we can access and integrate all regions of our brain and commence the healing and vertical development journey.

Up next, I will use my vertical development journey to illustrate the principles covered thus far.

CHAPTER SEVENTEEN

MY VERTICAL DEVELOPMENT JOURNEY

Vertical Development Law #17
There is no organizational transformation without a preceding transformation in the vertical development of the organization's leaders.

What does it look and feel like to develop vertically and upgrade your internal operating system? Allow me to share my journey.

MIND 1.0

From around age eighteen, when I entered adulthood, until I was roughly thirty-five, I operated in Mind 1.0. My internal operating system was wired for safety, comfort, and belonging. For me, the group I looked to for my safety, comfort, and belonging was the religion I was raised in.

Jostling for position in the center of the penguin huddle where it feels most safe and comfortable, I sought to belong by doing everything my church asked of me. This ranged from the little things like regular prayer, Scripture study, church attendance, and paying tithes, to pushing pause on my college education at nineteen to serve a two-year mission for my church.

As a missionary, I tried my very best to obey all the rules of the mission and do all that was expected of me. After my mission, I continued to be very active and involved in my church as it still met my needs for safety, comfort, and belonging.

Looking back, I can see that I was a very **dependent thinker**. I did not want to be a leader, make decisions, or push back against my beliefs. I was comfortable allowing my church leaders to instruct me on what I should and should not do, and I was happy to do what I was told because my Mind 1.0 needs were being met.

As for my mindsets, I operated squarely from the limiting side of the equation. Here is how they showed up.

Entering college, I had wanted to become a medical doctor, so I signed up for the pre-med chemistry course. I ended up getting a C for that class—the lowest grade I had ever received. Looking through the lens of my **fixed mindset**, I saw this as an indication that chemistry was something that did not come naturally to me. Believing I could not improve my talents, abilities, and intelligence, I was convinced I would never be successful in future chemistry classes. And since chemistry is something one must get through to become a doctor, to me, this also meant I did not have what it takes to be a doctor. So I gave up on that dream and switched my major.

What gives away my **closed mindset** was my belief that for me to be safe, comfortable, and belong with my groups, I needed to be valued as an expert. This showed up the strongest in my religion and my profession as an academic.

As a missionary for my church, I effectively walked around all day, every day believing that what I believed was better than what those who were not of my faith believed. This prevented me from listening to and connecting with anyone outside of my faith.

And as an academic and teacher, I was convinced it was my job to know what was best. I was always quick to profess my knowledge. Whenever I was questioned or challenged by other researchers or my students, I would get defensive rather than ask questions and explore their perspectives.

I also had a strong **prevention mindset**. I approached my daily life by essentially asking how I could navigate the day in the most comfortable way possible.

What's more, I had a huge aversion to risk. I had been raised to view debt as something that should be avoided at all costs and that being an entrepreneur meant taking on risks that might put one's family in harm's way. So I graduated with my undergraduate and doctoral degrees without taking on any student debt, and I had no desire to ever start a business of my own.

Out of the four limiting mindsets, the one that was the strongest was my **inward mindset**, which showed up as a common thread in various domains of my life.

On sports teams, I only cared about *my* success, not the success of the team. As a missionary, I cared more about how I was viewed by my peers than about creating value for others. As an academic, I struggled to support others' ideas simply because they were not *my* ideas. In my interactions with others, I believed they were not doing their best. This made me quick to be critical of them rather than kind, understanding, and compassionate.

Through and through, my internal operating system was wired to protect my safety, comfort, and belonging.

SHIFTING FROM MIND 1.0 TO MIND 2.0

My shift from Mind 1.0 to Mind 2.0 started when I was about twenty-nine years old. It occurred in two phases.

Phase One

As a part of my religious involvement, I served my local congregation in a volunteer capacity as a financial and membership clerk. In this position, I attended all meetings associated with the leadership of the congregation. My primary responsibility was to take minutes at these meetings, which were mostly about the organization and operation of the congregation.

There was another type of meeting—called a disciplinary council—that occurred only in unique circumstances. Whenever such a council was called, I was required to attend and take minutes.

In my church, a disciplinary council occurred when a member of the congregation did something contrary to the rules of the church. According to the rules of the church, this person had to meet with the three highest-ranking congregational leaders to determine whether that person could retain proper standing within the congregation.

The only people involved in these meetings were the person who broke the rules, the three congregational leaders, and the clerk. As the clerk, I was not allowed to participate in or even communicate during the meetings. I had very little interest in attending these disciplinary councils, but I did so because taking minutes at these events was a part of my assigned responsibilities.

In the span of two months, there were two disciplinary councils. In both cases, the accused were women who had sexual relationships outside of marriage, something explicitly forbidden by the church.

The only reason the leaders even knew of these relationships was that these women had confessed their actions to the congregational leader, something similar to confessions in the Catholic Church.

What transpired in these meetings appalled me. In both instances, the congregational leaders grilled the women about their sex life. The purpose of this questioning was to help the leaders determine the severity of their actions and whether the person should retain membership within the church. These were well-intended men doing what the church expected of them.

I was devastated for the accused women, though. They were isolated and anxious, and they were being asked to discuss with relative strangers actions they had significant shame over.

Next, the leaders had to judge the spiritual well-being of the women.

I felt conflicted. On one hand, I wanted to be devoted to my church and fulfill my responsibilities. This required me to stay silent. And on the other hand, I wanted to stop the meetings, put an end to the questioning, and help these women not feel so alone.

After each of these meetings, I carried this conflict within me. I wondered how my church and its leaders—both of which I believed were ordained by God—could engage in a practice that I found deplorable.

What compounded my experience was that my critical thinking skills were growing at the time, thanks to the doctoral program I was in. This resulted in a full-fledged faith crisis. On the surface, I kept going to church and fulfilled my responsibilities. Inwardly, though, I was wrestling. I began questioning the beliefs I had held my entire life.

What I did not recognize at the time was that this faith crisis was not necessarily a *crisis* at all. What these disciplinary councils did for me was nudge me away from being a Mind 1.0 dependent thinker to starting to become a Mind 2.0 **independent thinker**. Until that time, I had largely accepted my religious beliefs without questioning, and I was now in a position where I felt I needed to figure out what I really believed.

Over the next five years, I wrestled with my faith. Eventually, I was able to come to a place where I felt emotionally and spiritually comfortable retaining certain beliefs that I found of value while developing new beliefs that were independent of some of the mainstream beliefs held by my religion.

I am still navigating what my relationship with my church looks like, and I am not sure where my relationship with it will go in the future. At the moment, I am comfortable wading into the uncertainty.

Phase Two

It was toward the end of this five-year journey of wrestling with my faith that I experienced another jostling in my life. At the time, I had stepped away from my academic position to try my hand at a career in consulting with Gallup.

After only eleven months at Gallup, I was laid off. This came after a conversation with my manager. I felt I had been pigeonholed into a position that I did not sign up for and was asking them to either expand my role or move me into a different role. They were unwilling to accommodate my request and thought it would be better if we parted ways.

At the time, I felt lost and discouraged. I never imagined I would find myself fired from a job, and I felt that by getting fired, I was letting down my wife, my children, and myself.

Fortunately, I had taken a leave of absence from my university, and I was able to go back without any issue. As someone who does not like to feel negative emotions, I suppressed my feelings by throwing myself into my research the two months before the fall semester started.

The research I had been working on was pointing toward mindsets, but this was not a topic I knew much about at the time. So, I spent the next two months doing a literature review on mindsets.

As the mindset framework—the one I describe in Chapter Fifteen—started taking shape, I could not help but consider the quality of my mindsets. Having recently been fired, I was in a mental space where I was willing to be brutally honest with myself. What I discovered was that I had all four of the limiting mindsets I described in the previous section.

Shifting My Mindsets. Having deepened my self-awareness around my mindsets, I naturally wanted to shift them, so that is what I focused on. For me, developing three of the four positive mindsets took some effort, but I was able to make these shifts rather easily.

To develop a **growth mindset**, it was simply a matter of recognizing there was a difference between fixed and growth mindsets and learning what a growth mindset was. The more I learned, the more I came to believe I could change my talents, abilities, and intelligence and that challenges and failures were not things to be avoided; they were things that accelerated my growth and development.

This increased understanding brought with it a broader **window of tolerance** for not being great at something the first time I tried it. In turn, this provided the cognitive and emotional bandwidth to start approaching **learning zone challenges** with greater readiness.

Regarding the development of an **open mindset**, I felt like I had gotten a head start wrestling with the cognitive dissonance associated with my religious experiences. More than any other, that experience taught me some valuable lessons. It taught me that my mind bucket was not as full as I thought it was, nor will it ever be full. It also taught me there are always more perspectives than my own, and the more I explore the perspectives of others, the greater my capacity to find truth and think optimally.

For me, the key to developing a **promotion mindset** was to use something called *The Five-Minute Journal*. Among other prompts, this journal offers daily opportunities to respond to questions such as:

- What are three things that would make today great?
- What are three amazing things that happened today?

This daily exercise helped activate and strengthen my promotion mindset neural connections. It did not take long for me to shift from a focus on wanting to skate by in the most comfortable way to a focus on how I could create the life of my dreams. Of all the mindset changes, this shift came the quickest.

The shift that has been the hardest for me has been developing an **outward mindset**. While I was making large shifts in other mindsets, I was only making incremental shifts toward an outward mindset. For one thing, I had a greater ability to examine whether I was being inward- or outward-minded, and this helped me keep myself in check, but I still found myself stuck on the inward mindset side of the continuum more than I cared to admit. Making a transformational shift would not come until I did some deeper work.

The Culmination of the Two Phases

Looking back, it seems clear to me now that my shift from Mind 1.0 to Mind 2.0 came primarily through engaging in top-down approaches to my vertical development. On the religious front, I was wrestling with cognitive dissonance and pushing against long-held beliefs. On the mindset front, I was awakening to my negative mindsets and consciously working on shifting them.

This process was not easy. In fact, it was a heavy cognitive and emotional struggle. I felt like a child who was learning how to do the monkey bars. I had already grabbed hold of the first bar with both hands and let my feet dangle below me. That bar represented my beliefs, perspectives, and mindsets that felt right, safe, and a part of my identity.

I was holding tightly to my beliefs, perspectives, and mindsets, but I also awakened to the fact that the goal of the monkey bars was not to simply hang there, but to cross to the other side. I faced a scary proposition: to move forward, I would have to let go with one hand to grab the next bar. But letting go was scary. After all, if I let go, I might fall and get hurt. So, much of my struggle dealt with the uncertainty of what might happen if I let go of what felt safe and let go of who I thought I was.

Ultimately, I had to get to the cognitive and emotional state where I was willing to let go, craft a new version of myself, and be okay with the chance of falling. Through this struggle, I was able to shift from being a dependent thinker to being more of an independent thinker.

I was also able to move past my needs to be safe, comfortable, and feel like I belonged. In fact, I upgraded my internal operating system to Mind 2.0 and became willing to be unsafe, uncomfortable, and not belong so I could cross the monkey bars and reach my new promotion-minded goals and desires.

MIND 2.0

Unsurprisingly, I started to operate very differently after my operating system upgrade. I was no longer focused on staying safe and comfortable. I became ambitious and goal-centered. I started to feel less like the passenger and more like the driver of my life. I was now on a mission to create a brighter future for myself and my family.

With this new internal programming, possibilities that I would have previously avoided started to make sense. I became willing and interested in writing a book (which became *Success Mindsets*). I also became interested in becoming an entrepreneur as a way to reach my goals, so I started my consulting practice. I became willing to acquire debt to get the business off the ground and grow my brand as a leadership development consultant.

For several years, my Mind 2.0 internal operating system drove me to continually focus on elevating my brand recognition and the quantity and quality of my consulting engagements. I wanted to stand out, advance, and create a higher-level lifestyle for myself and my family. It was a bonus that I was in a position to help leaders and organizations along the way.

SHIFTING FROM MIND 2.0 TO MIND 3.0

After a few years in Mind 2.0, I began to learn about vertical development. As I mentioned in Chapter Eight with the penguin analogy, I was quick to convince myself that I operated in Mind 3.0. But that was not the case.

I would not come to fully appreciate just how far I was from Mind 3.0 until I started EMDR and IFS therapy.

At the time that I began meeting with my therapist, I did not believe I had any trauma in my background. There were no divorces and no abuse. To me, there was nothing in my past I could identify as being traumatic. That would soon change.

As my therapist and I began doing a combination of EMDR and IFS and I picked up on the different parts of myself, we discovered I had some strong protectors within me that were trying to keep something safe and hidden from my consciousness.

As we continued the work and dug deeper, my walls came down. With the help of my therapist, I was able to identify two instances of trauma that I had written off as not being a big deal. While these instances are minor compared to what others may have lived through, it became very clear that these traumatic events had left their psychological mark on me.

What I found fascinating was that even though these events occurred in my past, their effects on my life were very much felt in the present. The events were perpetually pulling me toward self-protection and ultimately hampering my growth.

Discovering these instances, sitting with them, and appreciating the impact they had on my life caused me to change the stories I tell about myself, my parents, and my past.

Awakening to My Trauma

The first instance we discovered was an event that took place when I was about five years old. My parents had gotten into a shouting match. Memories from that day are still incredibly vivid to me. I remember watching from my bedroom as my dad took out a suitcase and started packing it while still arguing with my mom. Five-year-old me was convinced my dad was leaving us. I remember being incredibly frightened and bawling hysterically.

While seeing my parents argue and my dad pack his bags certainly was stressful, what I realized through EMDR was that the event itself was not what was the most traumatic. What was more traumatic was that neither of my parents came to comfort me. I was left to try to make sense of the situation by myself. I was left alone with my fear and sadness while my parents went on as if nothing had ever happened.

One of the reasons why this was such a pivotal experience in my life is that it sent a clear and early message that I could not count on my parents to be with me emotionally. When it came to meeting my emotional needs, I was on my own.

This was perpetuated in the second instance of trauma. This time, I was ten. A couple of days after my birthday, my brother-in-law—who was like a brother to me—had a seizure, and the circumstances around the event left him unable to breathe. By the time someone found him and called 911, he had been without oxygen for twenty minutes and was brain-dead.

For several days he was kept alive, hooked up to machines to see if there was any hope of survival, but once that did not seem possible, my sister had to make the difficult decision to turn off the machines.

The night he passed away, my parents were the ones who told me the news. I remember covering myself with a blanket and crying for about two hours.

What I learned through EMDR was that the most impactful part of this traumatic event was not the death of my brother-in-law; it was the fact that I could not recall my parents comforting me. They did not hug me. They did not try to hold me. They did not ask if I was okay. They just sent me to bed.

There is no time in my life I felt more alone than I felt that night. For me, this was just another instance that sent the message that when it comes to my emotional needs, I was on my own.

Through this therapeutic process, I discovered several things that I had not realized before:

- I had, indeed, experienced trauma in my life. While I had not experienced abuse, I had experienced neglect, something that trauma researchers have discovered can have psychological effects as bad, if not worse, than those of physical abuse.

- I awakened to something I had been unwilling to see—I was an "alone person" living in an "alone body." While I have avoided seeing this aloneness in myself, I believe the people I have associated with throughout my life have been able to see and feel it. Coming to this realization of my internal aloneness, I could clearly see where my initial Mind 1.0 desires to stand in with my group came from, and later, where my Mind 2.0 desires to stand out came from. Standing in and standing out were two different ways I tried to fill the void within me caused by my aloneness.

- I could now see why shifting from an inward mindset was so difficult for me. From an early age, I had been taught that I was on my own when it came to meeting my emotional needs. Looking out for myself was a survival mechanism.

Ultimately, I could clearly see that my internal emotional aloneness was holding me back from fully moving into Mind 3.0. It would not be until I healed my mind that I would be able to shift into Mind 3.0.

STEPPING INTO MIND 3.0

While I am not sure I am fully in Mind 3.0 yet, and I know I do not yet spend 100 percent of my time there, I am stepping into Mind 3.0 more and more.

Through the bottom-up approaches of EMDR and IFS therapy, I have been able to deepen my self-awareness, reprocess my trauma, and improve my relationship with myself. This has felt like healing.

I no longer carry around the void of aloneness like I used to. I feel lighter, more centered, and more present. I have also made a significant positive shift in my outward mindset, and I feel as though I am seeing the world from a higher altitude.

The evidence of my vertical development progress includes:

- Having an improved relationship with my wife.
- Starting to strategize about the future of my business in new and elevated ways.
- Being more present with my children.
- Being more trusting of others.
- Being more focused on contributing and adding value to the world.
- Being more willing to step out of my comfort zone and into uncertainty.
- Seeing more of the Mind 3.0 characteristics within me, including greater emotional intelligence, psychological flexibility, intellectual humility, and infinite-mindedness.

But as I am strategizing about my future and stepping out of my comfort zone, I also feel the pull of self-protection. It is a helpful reminder that I still have room to elevate, but then again, that will always be the case.

DRILLING DEEP TO ELEVATE

One of the truths I have realized through my journey is that the deeper I have drilled and the more introspective I have been, the more I have elevated vertically. I invite you to also take steps to drill deep, heal, and elevate. It may help to decide if you will use a top-down approach, a bottom-up approach, or both.

If you will be using a top-down approach, focus on your mindsets. Identify one mindset that you want to focus on. It is impossible to master a mindset you know little about, so become an expert in that mindset.

Then, implement daily habits to activate and strengthen your positive mindset neural connection. The Digital Vertical Development Coach should already be helping you with this.

If you will be using a bottom-up approach, start with body-scan meditations and read books on trauma and healing. Also, seek out a trauma therapist who can help you strengthen your mind–body connection, foster integration, improve your encoding abilities, and widen your window of tolerance so you can elevate to contribution mode rather than be stuck in self-protection or self-focused reward mode.

Never forget, at a foundational level, vertical development is about healing your mind.

* * *

While it is great for us as leadership development professionals to work on and experience our own vertical development, you may also want to explore what you can do to help others develop vertically. That is where we are going next.

CHAPTER EIGHTEEN

THE RISING TIDE THAT LIFTS ALL SHIPS

Vertical Development Law #18
*The most effective way to shift the altitude of an organization
is to shift the vertical altitude of its executive team by elevating
their cognitive and emotional sophistication.*

When leaders develop vertically, they create a rising tide that lifts all ships. To demonstrate this, let us compare and contrast well-known Mind 2.0 leaders with well-known Mind 3.0 leaders.

Unfortunately, we do not have to look far to find leaders whose Mind 2.0 internal operating systems drive them to operate in a manner that leaves a wake of destruction. Some examples that come to mind include Travis Kalanick (co-founder and former CEO of Uber), Steve Ballmer (former CEO of Microsoft), Jack Welch (former CEO of GE), Kenneth Lay (former CEO of Enron), and "Chainsaw" Al Dunlap (former CEO of Scott Paper and Sunbeam).

Each of these leaders was once hailed as being great. But in hindsight, the aftermath of their Mind 2.0 leadership was catastrophic. Quotes associated with these leaders may give you a sense of their Mind 2.0 leadership and their strong focus on self and the competition.

- Travis Kalanick: "At Uber, we say, 'Always be hustling.'"

- Steve Ballmer: "My children, in many dimensions they're as poorly behaved as many other children, but at least on this dimension I've got my kids brainwashed: You don't use Google, and you don't use an iPod."
- Jack Welch: "Number one, cash is king . . . Number two, communicate . . . Number three, buy or bury the competition."
- Kenneth Lay: "I take full responsibility for what happened at Enron. But saying that, I know in my mind that I did nothing criminal."
- Al Dunlap: "People love comparing my $101 million against the 11,200 Scott Paper workers who were laid off on my watch. But the two totals are unrelated. The jobs were eliminated because the company couldn't afford them."

Finding Mind 3.0 leaders is more difficult. Fortunately, we do have some good examples to look up to, including Satya Nadella (CEO of Microsoft), Ed Catmull (former president of Pixar and Disney Animation), Alan Mulally (former CEO of Ford), and Frances Hesselbein (former CEO of Girl Scouts of America). Quotes associated with these leaders may give you a sense of their Mind 3.0 leadership and their strong focus on contribution. Can you see Mind 3.0 mentality in some of their more popular quotes?

- Satya Nadella: "I truly believe that each of us must find meaning in our work. The best work happens when you know that it's not just work, but something that will improve other people's lives."
- Ed Catmull: "The way I see it, my job as a manager is to create a fertile environment, keep it healthy, and watch for the things that undermine it."
- Alan Mulally: "Leadership is moving from *I* to *we* and *me* to *service*."
- Frances Hesselbein: "Work is love made visible." And "Leadership is a matter of how to be, not how to do."

My perception of these sets of leaders is that the Mind 2.0 leaders wanted to stand out and were comfortable using and burning out others to help them do so, while the Mind 3.0 leaders wanted to lift and elevate the people they led.

Once you study Mind 3.0 leaders, you will find that one of the characteristics that led to them creating a rising tide is they adopted a gardener mentality.

A GARDENER MENTALITY TO VERTICAL DEVELOPMENT

Expert gardeners understand three things:

- They do not have the power or ability to make a seed germinate, a plant grow, a flower bloom, or a tree bear fruit.
- If they want a seed to germinate, a plant to grow, a flower to bloom, or a tree to bear fruit, the gardener must create the right conditions for these things to occur.
- If they want the most seeds to germinate, the plants to grow quickly, the flowers to bloom most beautifully, and the trees to produce the most fruit, they must optimize the conditions for these things to occur based upon the type of plant or tree they are dealing with.

The same applies to helping others develop vertically. We cannot force vertical development onto others. We do not have that power or ability. But what we can do is provide the conditions that bring about vertical development.

Too often, though, when we try to help leaders change or develop, we address their limitations or shortcomings directly. We identify defects in their knowledge, skills, or competencies and try to address those. We try to fix the leader. And we tend to do so using horizontal development.

To help leaders elevate, our primary focus should not be on the leaders themselves. Instead, our first focus should be on the conditions that the leader is operating within and whether those conditions are ideal for growth and producing fruit—just like a plant.

This means that we need to create an environment that limits leaders' need to self-protect. We need to do our best to remove fear and threats to the leaders' needs and foster an environment where they can contribute, elevate, and lift others. It is only after we create the right conditions that we should focus on the leaders.

Creating the Right Conditions

In my study of the Mind 3.0 leaders described throughout, I have found that they focus on three foundational elements that create the right conditions for vertical development to occur.

These elements are developing a clear, inspirational, and stakeholder-centric purpose, developing clear values and lovingly holding others accountable to them, and developing a psychologically safe space.

Develop a Clear, Inspirational, and Stakeholder-Centric Purpose. Mind 1.0 leaders generally do not have a clear purpose; instead, their focus is on doing what is easiest or the most comfortable. Whether Mind 2.0 leaders have a formalized purpose or not, their focus is generally on making progress and hitting certain performance outcomes.

In contrast to these, Mind 3.0 leaders' purposes are not to make progress, but to create value for all stakeholders. This purpose is focused outside of the leader and the organization and on contributing, lifting, and elevating others.

You get this sense when Frances Hesselbein (former CEO of Girls Scouts of America) says, "Work is love made visible."

Also, you get this sense of clear, inspirational, and stakeholder-centric purpose in the purpose statements that Mulally and Nadella developed at Ford and Microsoft:

- Ford: "Opening the highways to all mankind"
- Microsoft: "To empower every person and every organization on the planet to achieve more"

Catmull likewise exudes this sentiment when writing in *Creativity, Inc.*, "We realized that our purpose was not merely to build a studio that made hit films but to foster a creative culture that would continually ask questions."

For all these leaders, the focus was not on making progress, but on adding value.

Develop Clear Values and Lovingly Hold Others Accountable to Them. A purpose statement identifies the *why* behind what an organization does. But a clear set of values defines *how* they are going to fulfill that why.

It is not uncommon for Mind 1.0 leaders to create clear values, but their values are generally focused on safety, comfort, and belonging. They often have a strong family feel to them.

Mind 2.0 leaders either neglect developing values, or they only give lip service to them. To Mind 2.0 leaders, organizational values are seen as a potential obstacle to their ability to make progress.

But Mind 3.0 leaders understand that values are necessary to get everyone in the organization working toward accomplishing the purpose in ways that best contribute, add value, and lift. And they are consistently referring to these values as a way to ensure that they walk the walk.

Alan Mulally's number one value at Ford was "People first . . . love 'em up." Other values included, "Everyone is included," "Everyone knows the plan, the status, and areas that need special attention," "Respect, listen, help, and appreciate each other," "Emotional resilience—trust the process," and "Have fun, enjoy the journey and each other."

Mulally once told me he does not feel like he ever had to fire anyone. If someone was not living up to Ford's values, they were choosing to leave.

The values Catmull developed at Pixar and Disney Animation were very much in support of the purpose of ensuring a creative culture that produces movies audiences will love. These values included honesty, candor, embracing failure, and remedying any psychological fears, along with values statements such as "Conflict is healthy," "Change is our friend," "Embrace randomness," and "Uncover what is unseen."

I had quoted Catmull earlier as saying ". . . my job as a manager is to create a fertile environment, keep it healthy, and watch for the things that undermine it." With his gardener mentality, he saw his primary job as the conservator of these values.

Develop a Psychologically Safe Space. In my work with organizations, I have observed that because Mind 1.0 leaders like safety, comfort, and belonging, they develop a warm culture with a somewhat psycholog-ically safe environment provided staff stay aligned with the status quo. However, these companies tend *not* to be psychologically safe for staff who push against the status quo.

I have also observed that the most psychologically unsafe environments are led by Mind 2.0 leaders. In a recent call with a prospective client, I asked them to describe their culture. Their response was that it was "formal, seri-ous, look to bosses for decision-making, and conservative." Clearly, there is a lot of fear in this organization, likely because of its hard-driving Mind 2.0 leaders. While fear can get people to act, it is not a sustainable strategy in the long term, largely because it kills psychological safety.

It is Mind 3.0 leaders that prioritize psychological safety and create a truly psychologically safe environment. At Pixar and Disney Animation, to foster the psychological safety necessary for the highest levels of creativ-ity, Catmull created Braintrust meetings. These were safe-space meetings where feedback on a film could be delivered with candor and any ideas for improvement could be shared and be heard without fear of any ram-ifications.

At Ford, in an effort to turn the ship around, Mulally started having weekly business plan review (BPR) meetings with his executive team. In preparation for the first meeting, he instructed his executives to report on their business units by giving a red light (meaning they were off-plan), a yellow light (meaning they were moving toward being on-plan), or a green light (meaning they were on-plan).

At the first BPR, Mulally gave each executive a chance to report. As they went around the table, everyone gave green lights. This left Mulally scratching his head, wondering how Ford could be set to lose billions of dollars, yet everyone gave a green light on their unit's progress. He realized he still needed to earn their trust.

For weeks, all he got during BPRs were green lights, testing Mulally's patience. When Mark Fields, then-president of Ford Americas, pushed back the launch date of the new Ford Edge, he told one of the other exec-utives that he should probably give a red light at the upcoming BPR. The executive responded, "It's been nice knowing you," symbolizing just how psychologically unsafe the culture at Ford had been prior to Mulally.

At the next BPR, Fields mustered up the courage to report a red light, to which Mulally stood up and clapped. Later, Mulally's executives told him that when he stood up and clapped, they all thought it was a signal for the board room doors to fly open and security to come and usher Fields out. *That* is how psychologically unsafe Ford's culture was.

But for Mulally, that moment was "one of the most important moments in the turnaround of Ford." To him, it was a ray of hope that they could turn the company around. It was only when the executives were willing to admit they had problems that they could do something about those problems.

* * *

While the order of addressing a company's purpose, values, and psychological safety can be debated—and it is a great debate to have—I present them in the order that I did for the following reasons.

I believe that purpose needs to come first. This is because it is critical that we get leaders' and employees' eyes off themselves and onto something external to themselves. Being clear on your purpose is critical for doing that.

Once their eyes are on something other than themselves, they can better focus on identifying values that support the purpose and create the space for dialogue stemming from different perspectives. Purpose and values become the filter for all decision-making passes.

Psychological safety is important for the process of developing a clear, inspirational, and stakeholder-centric purpose along with clear values, but it is hard to create an environment that is truly psychologically safe without the clear focus that a purpose brings and without the clear boundaries that values bring.

With a clear, inspirational, and stakeholder-centric purpose, clear values, and psychological safety, transformational and sustainable change can begin in the organization.

The transformation that occurred at Ford, Microsoft, and Disney Animation under Mulally, Nadella, and Catmull is nothing short of remarkable. But such transformation is only possible with a Mind 3.0 leader, someone who has the cognitive and emotional sophistication to lay the right foundation. And this comes from them having a gardener mentality that creates the conditions for vertical development to occur.

HOW TO HELP OTHERS DEVELOP VERTICALLY

When I work with organizations on top-down approaches, I always start with awareness. I inform leaders and employees of vertical development and the three mind levels so they can get a sense of where they are, where they need to go, and why.

Next, I introduce them to mindsets and help them not only put labels to mindsets, but also awaken to their current mindsets. Again, I am helping them become aware of where they are and giving clarity about where they could go in their vertical journey.

Becoming clear on the vertical development and mindset frameworks lays the foundation for the vertical development journey to begin.

Then, I create programming to activate and strengthen the leaders' and employees' positive mindset neural connections. This can include workshops, coaching, digital tools like the Digital Vertical Development Coach, and the development of personal vertical development plans. (Visit www.ryangottfredson.com/vertical-development-resources for more information.)

I am not qualified to engage in many bottom-up approaches, but I do think that organizations, as a part of their benefits packaging, could do a better job of providing access to trained trauma therapists to help bring healing. I imagine that organizations would be much more value-creating for all stakeholders if executives engaging in trauma therapy was normalized.

Bringing Trauma into the Workplace

Another approach is to help organizational leaders become more trauma-informed, helping them understand what trauma is, what the dominoes of trauma are, and what the effects of these dominoes are.

There are at least three benefits of becoming trauma-informed leaders:

- It helps us to be more compassionate and less critical of others. Instead of thinking, "What is wrong with them?" when someone is being overly self-protective or lacking emotional intelligence, you will find yourself asking, "What happened to them?" This empowers us to bring greater heart into the workplace.

- It helps us make decisions about the benefits and development that will elevate our company culture and employees such that the organization becomes less fear-inducing and more value-creating, which is essential for growth and long-term success. It would be inhumane to learn about trauma and not do more to address it.

- As individuals, the more trauma-informed we are, the greater our capacity to elevate ourselves. We will develop a greater capacity to sense our self-protective alarm bells, identify our mindsets, and name the feelings—both in our mind and body—when those alarm bells go off. We will also be more intentional about seeking healing.

* * *

When we as leaders elevate, so will our organizations. But it all starts with our vertical development. We must first work on ourselves, after which we can develop a gardener mentality, creating the conditions that allow for others to grow. This will raise the tide that lifts those around us.

From this chapter, three truths about vertical development become more readily apparent:

1. Regardless of our current altitude, we can always elevate.
2. The deeper we go inward and heal our minds, the higher we will elevate.

3. The more we do elevate, the greater positive influence we will have on the world around us.

Before turning to the final chapter, ask yourself:

- Am I operating with a gardener mentality?
- What can I do better to raise my tide and lift the ships around me?

CHAPTER NINETEEN

BECOME AN ELEVATED LEADER

Vertical Development Law #19

The more vertically developed leaders are, the more capable they are of leading successful change, and the more they recognize that organizational change starts with changing themselves.

There are three reasons why I wrote this book: I wanted to help you awaken to vertical development, an underutilized dimension of leadership development. I wanted to help you awaken to your current vertical altitude. And I wanted to help you awaken to how you can transform yourself as a leader and transform the leaders and people you work with.

AWAKENING TO VERTICAL DEVELOPMENT

Horizontal development has long been our go-to form of development. And while it should never go away, you now know it has severe limitations. Specifically, it does not address the root of the most pressing challenges that we and our organizations are facing.

Right now, most organizations are running on a leadership deficit. The change, pressure, uncertainty, and complexity that leaders are having to navigate exceeds their current abilities to deal with that change, pressure, uncertainty, and complexity. This results in well-intended but subpar and self-focused leaders that, at best, keep their boat afloat but do not make much progress, or, at worst, sink their boat and those still onboard.

Given that a leader's world is unlikely to decrease in change, pressure, uncertainty, or complexity, we need vertical development more than ever before. And we will continue to need it.

I hope you now feel clear on how you can upgrade your internal operating system to operate from a higher vertical altitude and how you can help others do the same so you and your organization can more effectively navigate the tumultuous environment we are currently facing and will continue to face.

The Primary Lesson of Vertical Development

In the process of writing this book and engaging in my own vertical development, there is one thing that has resonated with me most meaningfully, and that is that elevating our leadership, at its foundational level, is about healing ourselves.

I am hard-pressed to think of a more beautiful message than that. For me, this means I need to seek healing and restoration. And as a leadership developer, it means I can be a healer of minds, bodies, and hearts.

I wish the same for you. I wish healing for you. I also trust that you will elevate to become a gardener within your sphere of influence, creating the environment that fosters the healing and growth of others.

The reality is that each of us carries around our own trauma-related wounds and sensitivities that, if left unaddressed, restrain us. Left unhealed, the neurological wiring associated with

> Elevating our leadership, at its foundational level, is about healing ourselves.

these wounds and sensitivities limits our cognitive and emotional sophistication and causes our internal operating system to hold tightly to our core self-focused needs, and it prevents us from being the positive influence we desire to be. But we can heal, and we can elevate.

I am excited about your vertical development journey. I am excited for you to not only become more of an interdependent thinker, but to develop more of the characteristics of those who operate in Mind 3.0. My wish for you is that you will become more

- emotionally intelligent;
- centered, mindful, and present;
- a systems thinker;
- learning goal-oriented;
- focused on your purpose;
- intellectually humble;
- psychologically flexible; and
- infinite-minded.

By operating at this vertically developed level and possessing these characteristics, I do not think it is far-fetched to think we can create a massive rising tide that elevates the world.

RESOURCES FOR YOUR JOURNEY

One of the things I have enjoyed with my family is visiting various national parks, with Yosemite National Park in California being a favorite. When we were there, we went on several hikes with varying degrees of difficulty. On one of the longer hikes, I remember thinking, *I am so grateful for really clear direction signs.* Because of the signs, I was able to explore the rugged wilderness of Yosemite without stressing about being on the right track.

I do not know about you, but my vertical development journey has certainly felt like exploring a rugged wilderness at times. It has been helpful to have some direction signs along the way—books on the topic. In fact, other than therapy—which is like having a personal guide in the wilderness—I have found books to be the most helpful resource on my journey.

I may go so far as to say it is impossible to develop vertically without engaging in deep learning, without exposing ourselves to ideas that push against our current perspectives and beliefs.

Thus, I would like to share with you the books I have found to be the most helpful along my journey thus far. I only include books I have read.

If you would like to keep up to date with my recommendations, you can sign up for my weekly newsletter at www.ryangottfredson.com/blog.

GENERAL VERTICAL DEVELOPMENT BOOKS
- *Positive Intelligence* by Shirzad Chamine
- *Loving What Is* by Byron Katie
- *Deep Change* by Robert E. Quinn
- *The Learning Landscape* by James Anderson
- *The Boy, the Mole, the Fox, and the Horse* by Charlie Mackesy
- *Immunity to Change* by Robert Kegan and Lisa Lahey

MINDSET BOOKS
- *Bonds that Make Us Free* by Terry C. Warner
- *Think Again* by Adam Grant
- *Leadership and Self-Deception* by The Arbinger Institute
- *The Anatomy of Peace* by The Arbinger Institute
- *The Infinite Game* by Simon Sinek
- *You are a Badass* by Jen Sincero
- *Lift* by Ryan W. Quinn and Robert E. Quinn

TRAUMA HEALING BOOKS
- *What Happened to You?* by Bruce D. Perry and Oprah Winfrey
- *The Body Keeps the Score* by Bessel van der Kolk
- *The Deepest Well* by Nadine Burke Harris
- *The Boy Who Was Raised by a Dog* by Bruce D. Perry
- *Calm Clarity* by Due Quach
- *The Gifts of Imperfection* by Brené Brown

BOOKS ON THE MIND
- *Mindsight* by Daniel J. Siegel, MD
- *Seven and a Half Lessons About the Brain* by Lisa Feldman Barrett
- *The Brain that Changes Itself* by Norman Doidge

LEADERSHIP BOOKS RELATED TO VERTICAL DEVELOPMENT

- *Creativity, Inc.* by Ed Catmull
- *The Motive* by Patrick Lencioni
- *Principles* by Ray Dalio
- *Dare to Lead* by Brené Brown
- *Leadershift* by John Maxwell
- *The Go-Giver* by Bob Burg and John David Mann
- *I Hear You* by Michael Sorensen

PARENTING BOOKS THAT PROMOTE VERTICAL DEVELOPMENT

- *The Conscious Parent* by Shefali Tsabary
- *The Awakened Family* by Shefali Tsabary

BIOGRAPHIES OR MEMOIRS BY THOSE WHO HAVE VERTICALLY DEVELOPED

- *The Choice* by Edith Eger
- *The Gift* by Edith Eger
- *A Long Walk to Freedom* by Nelson Mandela
- *Unfollow* by Megan Phelps-Roper
- *Educated* by Tara Westover
- *Can't Hurt Me* by David Goggins
- *Hollywood Park* by Mikel Jollett
- *The Autobiography of Martin Luther King, Jr.* by Martin Luther King, Jr. (I recommend listening to this one)

DEEP-THINKING BOOKS THAT HAVE PUSHED MY COGNITIVE AND EMOTIONAL SOPHISTICATION

- *Sapiens* by Yuval Noah Harari
- *Lost Connections* and *Chasing the Scream* by Johann Hari
- *The Righteous Mind* by Jonathan Haidt
- *A New Earth* by Eckhart Tolle

- *The Art of Possibility* by Rosamund Stone Zander and Benjamin Zander
- *Talking to Strangers* and *David and Goliath* by Malcolm Gladwell
- *Just Mercy* by Bryan Stevenson
- *The Moment of Lift* by Melinda Gates
- *The Bottom of the Pool* by Andy Andrews
- *The Sin of Certainty* by Peter Enns
- *Bittersweet* by Susan Cain
- *Caste* by Isabel Wilkerson

ACKNOWLEDGMENTS

I have two children whom I love and am so incredibly grateful for. I remember anticipating their births with anxious excitement, not just for their arrival, but for what they might become in this world. I feel very similarly about the books I have written.

As I finish writing this book, I feel like I am about to give birth to a new child. I have anxious excitement for its release, but I am also curious about what this book might become in this world. And I am so incredibly grateful for two groups of people who have helped make this book a reality.

The first group of people is those who have helped me on my personal vertical development journey. My wife, Jena, for taking the journey with me. My children, Hailey and Spencer, for the inspiration to elevate as a father. My therapist, Patricia Torres, for helping me awaken and heal. My friends and colleagues, who include Alan Mulally, Amy Kelly, Chantale Ranger, Lisa Anna Palmer, Marcio Welter, Ralph Campbell, Rupert Reyneke, and Whitney Johnson, among others. And all of the people who have written the books I listed as resources. Each of you has left an indelible mark upon my soul.

The second group of people is those who have helped me make this book a reality. David Hancock and the team at Morgan James Publishing. My editor, Adéle Booysen. My proofreaders, Cortney Donelson and Alyssa Hanes with vocem LLC. Amber Vilhauer and her team at NGNG. My friends at Qstream who have been so gracious to provide you with the free Digital Vertical Development Coach. And Rupert Reyneke and the team at Red Stone Studio for elevating my digital presence.

Finally, to you, the reader, thank you for letting me be a part of your journey.

ABOUT RYAN

R yan Gottfredson, Ph.D. is a cutting-edge leadership development author, researcher, and consultant. He helps organizations vertically develop their leaders primarily through a focus on mindsets. Ryan is the Wall Street Journal and USA Today best-selling author of *Success Mindsets: The Key to Unlocking Greater Success in Your Life, Work, & Leadership*, and now, *The Elevated Leader: Level Up Your Leadership Through Vertical Development*.

He is also a leadership professor at the College of Business and Economics at California State University-Fullerton. He holds a Ph.D. in Organizational Behavior and Human Resources from Indiana University and a B.A. from Brigham Young University.

As a consultant, he works with organizations to develop their leaders and improve their culture (collective mindsets). He has worked with top leadership teams at CVS Health, Deutsche Telekom, and dozens of other organizations.

As a respected authority and researcher on topics related to leadership, management, and organizational behavior, Ryan has published over twenty articles across a variety of journals including Leadership Quarterly, Journal of Management, Journal of Organizational Behavior, Business Horizons, Journal of Leadership and Organizational Studies, and Journal of Leadership Studies. His research has been cited over 3,200 times since 2017.

A free ebook edition is available with the purchase of this book.

To claim your free ebook edition:

1. Visit MorganJamesBOGO.com
2. Sign your name CLEARLY in the space
3. Complete the form and submit a photo of the entire copyright page
4. You or your friend can download the ebook to your preferred device

Morgan James
BOGO™

A **FREE** ebook edition is available for you
or a friend with the purchase of this print book.

CLEARLY SIGN YOUR NAME ABOVE

Instructions to claim your free ebook edition:
1. Visit MorganJamesBOGO.com
2. Sign your name CLEARLY in the space above
3. Complete the form and submit a photo of this entire page
4. You or your friend can download the ebook to your preferred device

Print & Digital Together Forever.

Snap a photo

Free ebook

Read anywhere

Printed in the USA
CPSIA information can be obtained
at www.ICGtesting.com
JSHW022219140824
68134JS00018B/1149

9 781631 958915